On the Journey

To Maggie Jamison
Enjoy Your Journey!

Cynthia Thomas
1/8/14

On the Journey

The Art of Living with Breast Cancer

Illustrated and Written
By
Cynthia Thomas

Balboa Press books may be ordered through booksellers or by contacting:

Balboa Press
A Division of Hay House
1663 Liberty Drive
Bloomington, IN 47403
www.balboapress.com
1 (877) 407-4847

ISBN: 978-1-4525-9527-6 (sc)
ISBN: 978-1-4525-9528-3 (e)

Library of Congress Control Number: 2014905998

Printed in the United States of America.

Balboa Press rev. date: 5/1/2014

Cynthia's Artwork Photographed By Jim Fagiolo
Cover Design by Karin Anderson

BALBOA
PRESS
A DIVISION OF HAY HOUSE

This book is Dedicated to all the women living with breast cancer.
May we all win back our Health.

Acknowledgements of Gratitude: I want to share a special thanks to my loving husband, John Dach, who has put up all these years with this crazy, demanding, determined and possessed artist. For all his understanding and patience that he has shown me, especially while I have been On the Journey, through the mastectomy, radiation and recurrence and all the while, supporting me doing my artwork; I thank him for all his encouragement of my artwork even when he did not understand why or what I was doing. To all my family and friends: Thank you for being my anchors and rocks, supporting me throughout the Journey, with Angels, Love and Prayers; and thank you to all the Facebook® followers, who encouraged me to put this book together.

I want to give a special thanks to my dear friend Dana Driver, fellow artist and my traveling partner over the years, for all her loving support and encouragement.

A Special thanks to Susan Shaw for helping me choose from over 122 pastels which pastels to put in the book. I thank my friends Linda Chapman ATR BC, Linda Collins Chapman, Susan Burrescia, Suzanne Johnson, Tahaia Johnson, Dru Mogler and many more, for all their support. Each of you has given me so much through listening, your prayers, Angels and support.

I want to thank the "Studio by the Creek" artists for their loving encouragement and support: Dee Green, Diana Miller, Beth Taylor, Bettye TaBain, Irene Loghry, Barbara Van Vorst, Gayle Selby, Linda Parcell, Sandra Kasper and Deborah Hilt. I thank the artists at Gallery 9 who have been there for me as well. And to my valiant proofreaders: Kimberly Carroll, Judy Rhodes, Lynne Armstrong, Elise Daniels and John, for proof reading the pages so thoroughly.

I am very grateful for the cover design by Karin Anderson.

I could not have put the book together without all your help, encouragement and support.

I thank you all, from my heart and Soul.

The Process: Art has been my life. In 2006, I had a rough time. I was unable to create anything. The block was broken when I challenged myself to do a pastel drawing every day. The routine I developed was to write three pages every morning, inspired by <u>The Artist's Way</u> by Julia Cameron. I would do my prayers and gratitude list and then I present my Self to the white paper. My pastels are laid out like a rich rainbow in their carrying case. I reach for whichever color catches my attention. I then cover the entire sheet of paper with that color. It sets the tone for the morning's work.

I sought to understand what I was doing and why, and found that I was on a Chakra Journey. I studied the Chakra color energies to better understand them: 1st Chakra – Root – red, 2nd Chakra – Creativity/Sexuality- orange, 3rd Chakra – Solar plexus/Power – yellow, 4th Chakra- Heart/Love – green, 5th Chakra – Voice – bright blue, 6th Chakra – Third Eye/Insight – indigo blue, 7th Chakra – Crown/Thought – violet. Source/God/Higher Power is white. Often issues would come up and shine through the colors I picked that morning. I draw using lines, forms and colors. I rarely draw representational figures or scenes. I feel the energy and allow it to dictate the healing or the adjustments I need to make in my thinking.

My conscious goal is to move the toxic negative energies out of my body, mind and spirit and put the healing energies onto the paper. By moving the negativity out, I open my heart to the positive. At the heart of nearly all my mandalas, I bring in the Light. I begin with the pure connection to Source through my soul, my heart of hearts, where we all have this core of pure innocence connected to Source. The core can be deeply buried in the scar tissue of abuse, neglect, abandonment, etc. but it is there in each and every one's heart of hearts. Reaching the core enlightens us to our amazing power and the possibilities in Life.

Creating a discipline is the best way to start a creative journey. To engage in art five elements are needed, not necessarily in this order: discipline, focus, patience, mastery and faith. These are what I strive to achieve.

I do the Mandalas for my Self. It is the meditation I use to go deep in my soul to heal. The words are my way to share the Journey with others. Each person, on their own path, may find healing with the images and/or the words. It has been both an inner and an outer experience, putting words to what I was experiencing through the drawing. This is why I have shared the Journey with friends and now in this book, to the world.

Mandala: the definition: "symbol representing self: in Jungian psychology, a symbol representing the self and inner harmony". I use the circle for containment of my Self. I wish for each and everyone to achieve their path through whatever creative process works for them. This one works for me.

First Day On the Journey: Protective Cloud. The picture is the first of my Tumor pictures. Strange, it is the same shape as the cloud in my right eye from the retinal stroke last year. A lump was revealed: Right breast. I had a biopsy. Results found cancer. I am scheduled for a mastectomy. I am sorry to shock you. I am in a good place and after all the tests, so far, I am in good shape. Funny how, in light of all this, my priorities are rapidly shifting. The next weeks are full of stuff, things to do: paper and final for the graduate class I was taking; featured artist at Gallery 9 in Port Townsend, which includes finishing a couple of major new pieces and the First Saturday Art Walk; I was supposed to be the speaker at the local art guild, to name the big things. The "little stuff" is my job as a counselor and I have a number of private clients that I am seeing, besides the group I facilitate. So, I have got to clear my schedule and get this taken care of, heal, and resume where I left off.

Isn't life amazing? For some reason Hawaii, or Mexico, or Costa Rico, tropical places with quiet beaches and blue, warm water sound really good right now. Well, my way of handling the news was to pick up Ben and Jerry's Coffee Heath Bar Crunch for me, and a dozen roses for John. We ate ice cream, admired the roses and talked about all the "what's next" stuff. We talked about how I was going to tell whom. About my concern how our son, Michael would handle the news; how our daughter, Elise, might take it badly with her husband off fishing (his job); how my friends were going to take the news. "How" has been to just say it, how it is. I am having surgery then I will look at what is next, what the doctor says from the outcome of the surgery. One day at a time. Thank you for your prayers and positive energy. Thank you for ALL for your loving support. WOW! Such beautiful words, thoughts, offerings and love. It is the truest existential high; I feel this amazing sense of belonging. One cannot ask for more than that. I AM NOT ALONE! I share this love back to all of my friends and family.
Thank you All.

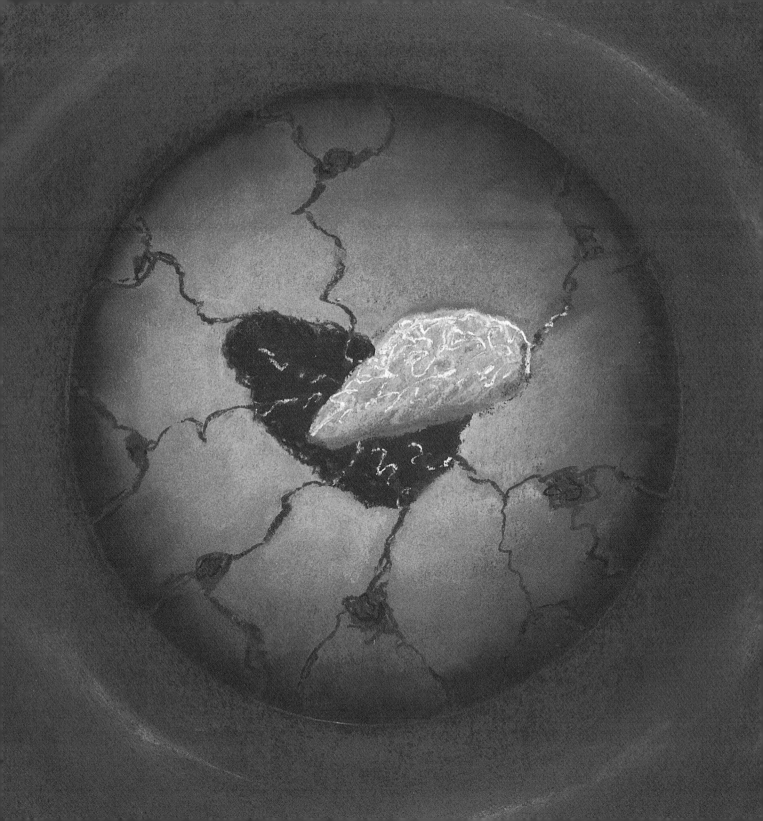

On the Journey: "Not So Twins". Yellow is the color for the Solar Plexus, Seat of Power. The clouds are part of the New Journey. I am so grateful for all the support, prayers and Angels I have received. I feel a marvelous sense of connectedness to all that is around me. Thank you. I have lots to do and am doing the best I can. Feeling the impending loss, feeling the need for some solitude and being with everyone, all at once. This process of decision-making that will affect my life, my health, and future in the most advantageous, highest, continuous quality of Life is really hard. My mind gets flooded with all the information and I work hard to stay focused on all the healthiest ways of coping with the stress. The different Doctors put their own type of pressures on me and don't always give me answers I can understand, or maybe that I don't want to hear. Though, at this time, as far as we all know, they will cut out all the cancer. The Radiology Oncologist will confirm that I am cancer free, to the best of her ability, with scans and whatever means she has available. Then we decide the best treatment path. I read two different studies that say the likelihood of the cancer recurring is at its highest in the next two years. Then the percentages for recurrence fall off rapidly to less and less likelihood of it recurring. The studies were done over a period of ten years. This is very heartening. These studies were with no treatment, and radiology only. So, I am reading and thinking and researching. I knew at completion of the piece that I needed to release this energy, let go of the feelings of confusion and know that what I need to learn is here. I am open to the best Path for me. The present is HERE, NOW. I am going to work for a while in the garden grounding myself in the earth! Enjoying the Sunny Days!! I do the art nearly everyday. The art has that quality of an interesting way of dealing with this recovering process. Strength is the lesson we learn when we really need it. Each day is special. Acceptance for What Is. Love for All That Is. Gratitude for All That Is. Thank you for being here!

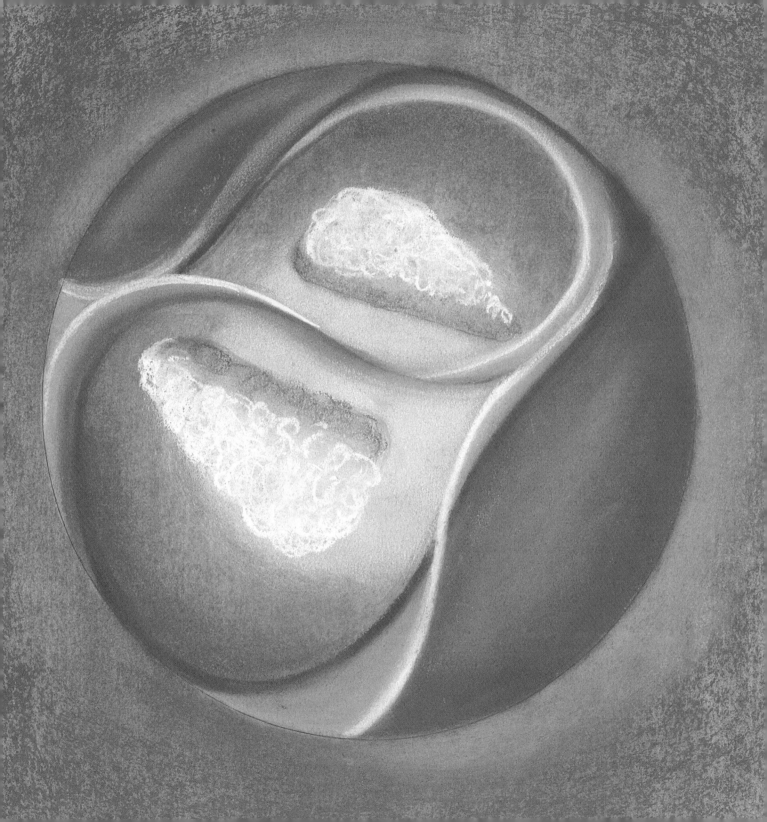

On the Journey: Insight Creativity. It really is a lovely piece. The biopsy aggravated my breast and it is uncomfortable. The surgery has been postponed a little. Ain't it grand. The surgeon fired me as a patient because I was too weird. I wanted the tissue back from the surgery for cremation, so it could later be joined with the rest of me when all my ashes are put in the ocean. He just couldn't handle that request. I have to start over with the new doctor. It is upsetting. The new surgeon is a woman and has no problem or issue with my request but she may not be able to schedule my surgery until, more likely, the following week. Recovery time is really not all that long, as I will be having nothing else done. So I need patience. Seems silly of me, to be so stubborn. No: Obdurate. It just is the way I am. I projected too much on the Doctor, thinking he would understand. Oh, Well. I am fine, just had to vent a bit. I want to make sure everyone understands this: I am not "bashing" the doctor. I am just disappointed. The doctor is being true to himself and I respect him and understand his position. I have to be true to me, too. A good solution has been arranged. I do have the highest respect for a person who stays true to their Self. Thank you ALL for your input. I grew up in medicine and know a lot more than the average person, how hard medical people work and the sacrifices they make for their passion. No bashing! Truly.

On the Journey: A Kind of Passage. So, we are on this Journey to the wonders of the inner self through the trials and challenges of cancer. I am soon to be cancer free once they do the surgery. The future path is better food, better self-care, less stress and more, much more, laughter in my life! Even better, I am here in my time and space. I reflect on that very issue. I am reading <u>Staring at the Sun</u> by Irvin Yalom. He discusses helping clients overcome the terror of death. Synchronistic, I got it before the diagnosis on the recommendation of a wise man. We all have this one-way ticket. We never know when it will be collected. So, for me, I am making the best of the time I have. I work at it. I enjoy something Every Day. I encourage everyone to do the same. One day at a Time. I go in at 6:30 in the morning for the surgery prep. Surgery is at 9:30. I was a bit blown away by the size of the tumor: 5.9 cm x 3.9 cm x 3.4 cm. The new Dr. is great, answered a lot of the questions I went in with before I even asked them. She had no problem with giving me the tissue once the lab is done with it. She had worked in the Southwest with the Navaho people and they cannot transition without all their parts. She completely understood. So it is a go. Enjoy today. There is always something fun, beautiful, and magical in every day.

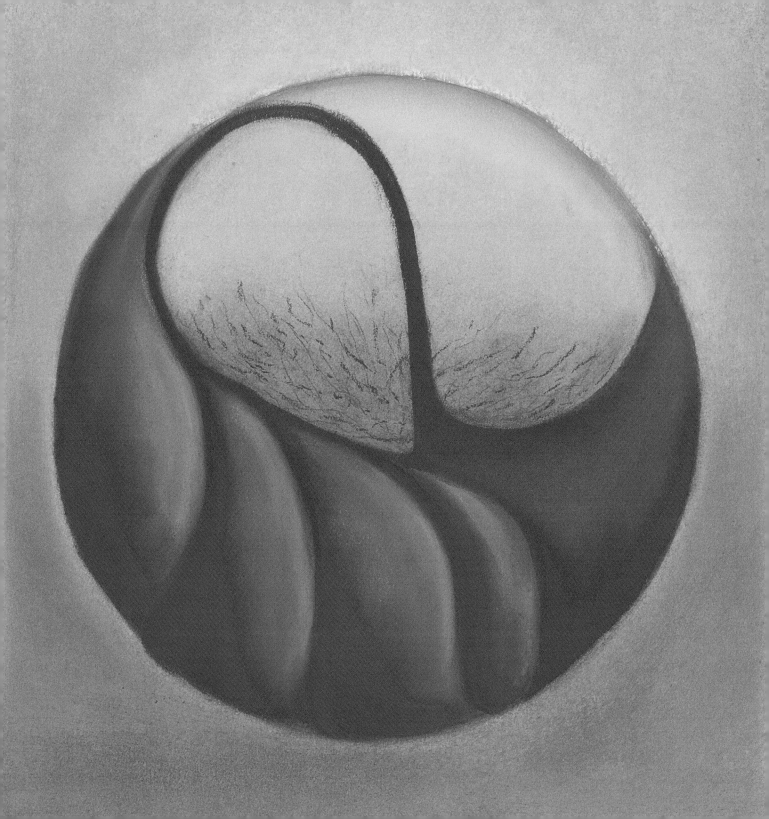

On the Journey: Masses. Well, I am home and "surgeried" (a new word.). I am sore and supposed to take it easy, like they say in the 12 Step Program: "Take it easy" or "Easy does it". Well, somehow that is going to have to fit into my vocabulary, somehow. I woke up at 6:00 AM, could not sleep any longer, and had to get the day going. I wrote in my journal and did this new piece. So, I will rest and "Take it Easy". Thank you for the support, Angels, and love. I am on the healing path. Some days are pancake days. Comfort food that may not be the best but is a reminder of the childhood treat when my dad would make pancakes on Sunday mornings. So, I flopped on the couch under a heap of blankets with the heating pad. I needed to go inside and heal. I needed to honor that place in me that wants to be coddled, pampered and rested. I feel so much better for the journey into the depths, and I am swimming in the reservoir of my strength, that has been fueled by all the support from friends, family and even strangers. Thank you for the loving thoughts. They strengthen me and fill me up.

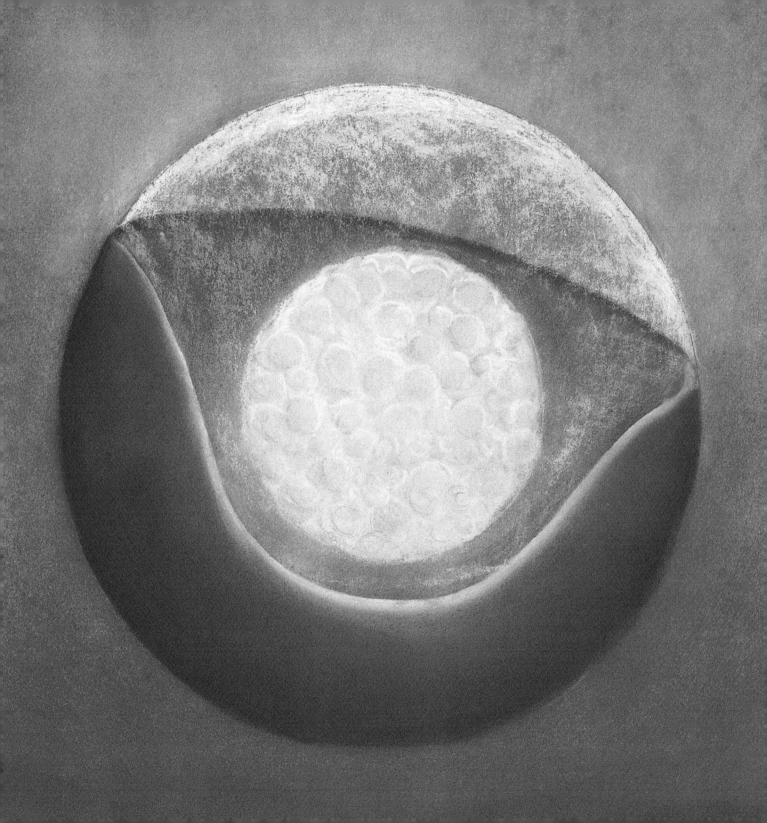

On the Journey: Rising. In this world of craziness, there is the light Rising. I hope everyone plays the little piece below and enjoys it as much as I do. It is the song "What doesn't kill you makes you stronger" sung by Kelly Clarkson and written by Jorgen Kjell Elofsson: https://www.facebook.com/photo.php?v=525615210792991&set=vb.100000335513629&type=2&theater. The song became my recovery chant On the Journey. I think we all need a "Fight Song" to rally the troops and inspire our healing. With all the Love and support that has been washing over me, I am healing in heart and soul, my mind and body are on the same path. I started out really tight and as I worked, things opened up. I think this is how I am on the Journey. It started really tight and it is opening up for me, more and more each day. For today, I am in perfect health. I am in perfect health. I allowed myself to get a little frazzled with printer issues and finally surrendered to waiting until I could talk to a human being. People are so much easier to deal with than the computer gibberish. I am grateful, and wish you all a solid day.

On the Journey: Pulse 108. I feel the healing in my body-mind-spirit. People have shared some amazing information for healing, through diet and spiritual support, and it helps keep my mind clear. Gratitude is the gift of today, the outpouring and Sisterhood, the love I am experiencing is beyond my wildest imagination. I know we all go around unaware of the love and acceptance that is in the air. Feel it. It is real; it is healing and I am grateful for the gift. With this path, I have discovered a fabulous community that is here for me any time. I am so grateful. Each day we face the trials and tribulations of life, we need to remember that we are not alone. We are in community every minute, whether we are aware of it or not. Being in the present is living in Peace. This is the goal. Here and Now. We are in the very best place we need to be, every moment. When we sit with that notion, life becomes amazing. So, present time is the peaceful place! Thank you all for being in my life and witnessing the Journey.

On the Journey: Intrusive Elements. Sometimes in the healing journey we encounter glitches that we have to investigate and confirm we are OK. Today was such a day. I am OK. Sometimes we question our own judgment. Sometimes we just need validation. I am OK. Still working in the 1st Chakra: Root: family, tribe, community, belonging. All good. I am learning to pay attention to the nuances of how I feel, and look at why. We went shopping at the grocery store. I did not realize it was rather late, well past lunchtime. I started getting snippy/snappy/impatient with my sweetie. Surely he deserved it, NOT. I was hungry. I was hungry, the now kind of hungry. Feed me, NOW. So when I finally realized it, I asked if he wanted something, no, he was fine (he had visions of a piece of pizza at Costco, but turned out they were closed). I went to the deli section in the market, ordered a tuna sandwich. We finished up, I ate the sandwich and felt tons better. I apologized for being snippy. I was just hungry. So simple, I could have checked in with me, my Self and I, and asked that question: What is going on in here? Am I: hungry, angry, lonely or tired: H.A.L.T. . #1, Bingo. I was in a feed me now getting grumpy state. Good question, when I feel snippy, grumpy, etc. to check out the H.A.L.T. list, 9 out of 10 times it is one of those minor issues that does NOT have to be blown out of proportion. I love lessons, reminders of what I already know. Now, especially now, I need to keep on task as to what is really happening in me. I think once in awhile things come up in the strangest ways. Being open to Source pushes images, colors and forms through to me. Sometimes they come really fast where I can barely grasp them; other times they meander through with all the time in the world. Regardless, I am blessed. Thank you all, you have no idea how much you contribute to this Path. I am ever so grateful for each and every one of you. Thank you.

On the Journey: An Out Pouring. Here is a part of the outpouring of gratitude I feel from all my friends and family. The richness of life is beyond words when we look at what we really have. When I do my morning writing I end it with a paragraph of gratitude: for the air I breathe, the cozy bed I sleep in, for the running hot and cold water, for the car I have put over a third of a million miles on and keeps going. I am grateful for the roof over my head, for the fact that no bombs are going off in the neighborhood, for my family being healthy, for my beautiful grandchildren. This is a small list. When times are hard for us, and we are feeling depressed and hopeless, we can STOP! Do a gratitude list, even with the simplest things like running water, air to breathe, and for the shoes on our feet. Doing a daily gratitude list helps us keep in perspective of what is really important, TODAY. We are here right now and we have these small comforts in our lives that many people around the world do not have. Reflect on all the things taken for granted in our lives, as in walking into a room and flipping on the light switch and we have light, turning on the faucet and there is water. Picking up the phone and calling a friend. Gratitude is an amazingly magical healer for the heavy heart. The mantra might be "I am ever grateful". Enjoy every day, as it is all we truly have when we open our eyes.

On the Journey: Perfect Health. The energy of perfect health flows through me and I am whole. End of Story. Some have thought I should be a wounded creature. Nope, I am ME. Whole. Capable. Interesting how powerful one feels when one lets go of others' wounded projections. It is hard to explain. I am feeling better than I have for a long time and on a myriad of levels in Body, Mind and Spirit. I live my life by this credo: I am the kind of woman who "when my feet hit the floor, the devil says 'Oh shit. She's up'.". It is the balance in our true self that brings balance in all aspects of our lives. When we are in balance the energy flows and we create the moment, through Source. It does not matter so much where I am physically, as where in me does the balance sit so the flow is most powerful for me. So I rest. I am serene and full of creative energy, all at once. I saw the surgeon with the results from pathology: Stage 3A, only one lymph node had metastatic carcinoma, which is good because it was taken out. I now am on the waiting path for the Oncology Office to set up an appointment. When I need a nap, I take one. I am also participating in a Healing Meditation. It is lovely, balancing and good for me. Enjoy every day; take naps when you need one! Amazing what rest does for the soul, along with a little meditation. I started in Balance as the mental theme today and the energy was very interesting. I ultimately needed definition and clarity, as I see it. So I go about my day with definition and clarity. I am serene and full of creative energy, all at once. Take walks, do art. Do your best every day. Have a Great Day.

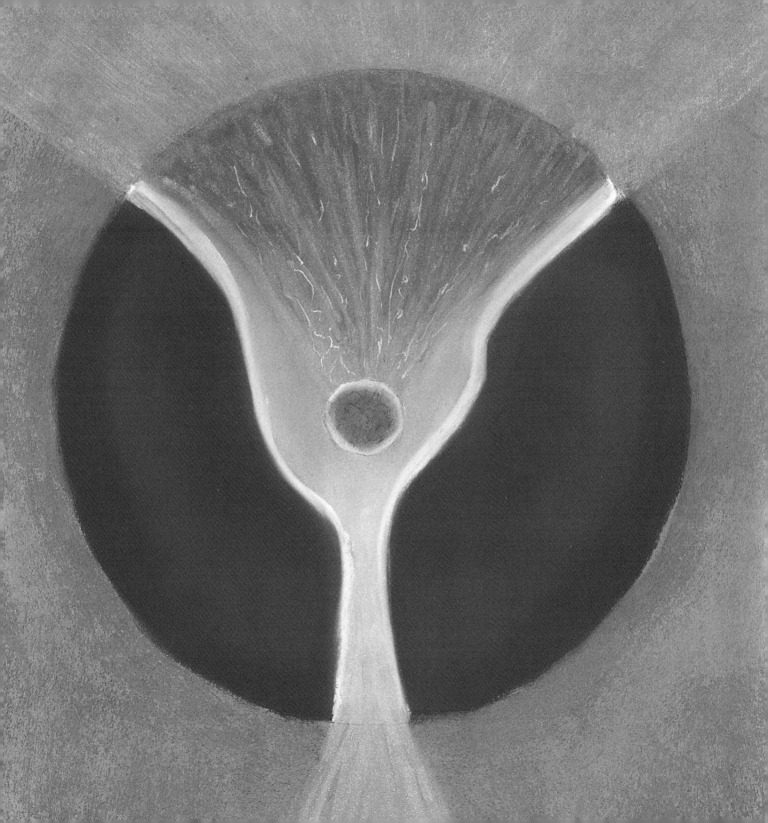

On the Journey: A Coming Together. The birds were out in the early dawn singing to their hearts' content. It was a great way to wake up. I took my walk today in the breezy cool weather. Felt really good to be outside in the air, moving. I enjoy walking, it helps me feel alive, connected and engaged. I walk three miles in about an hour, plus or minus. It is a nice pace for me. Exercise is also part of the healing process. Makes the heart work, makes the legs and body loosen up, clears the head and supports the immune system, along with naps and laughter. Oh yes, we don't want to leave out the good food. Life is so rich. And then I get to do art. Coming together, resting in the gravity of the Planet. I was inspired by an image I saw and played with it. The rest is the play on the shadow, our dark side. We all have the Light and Shadow in our psyche. The balance of the two is delicate. I can fall into the shadow if I am not vigilant. It is in the Light where we find the joy, Source, and are elevated in Spirit. In the Shadow, we fall prey to the "black and blue meanies" which can be most toxic. We cannot deny the Shadow; we must explore it, and expose it within ourselves. We should not allow it to hide in the dark recesses of our minds, as fermenting addiction, greedy, controlling, ugly, perverse, judgmental, rigid and self-serving thoughts. I think of the Shadow side as the place, in all of us where the seven deadly sins are derived. Fodder for thought. The wind is up again and I need to get on with my day. There is nothing like the beginning of each new day. Amazing what a little rest does for the soul, and a little meditation. I started in balance as the mental theme for the drawing and the energy was very interesting. Nap, laugh, eat good healthy food and exercise are on the menu. Enjoy.

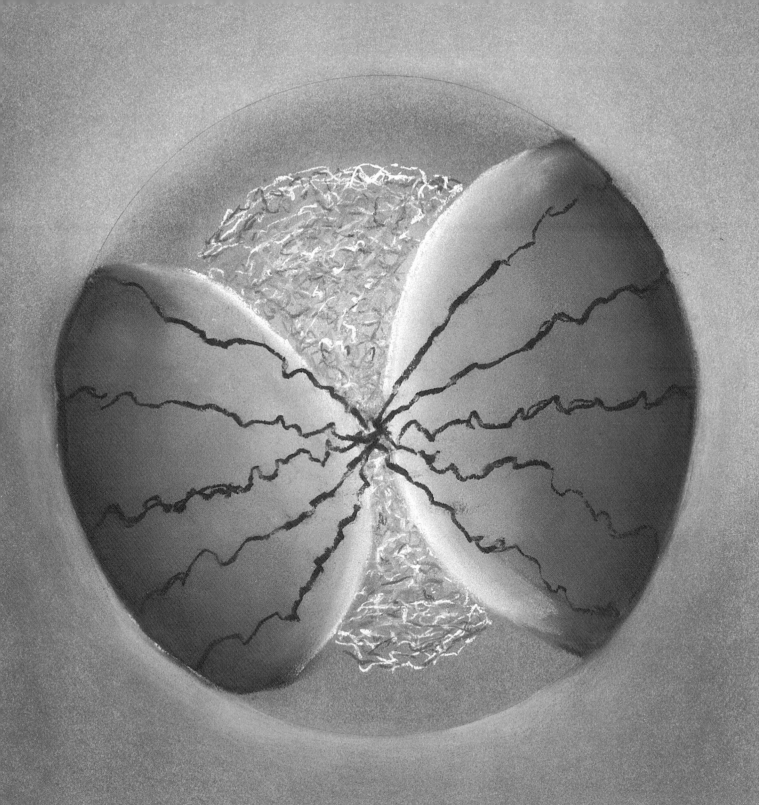

On the Journey: In Sync. I am working on being in sync in my Mind, Body, Spirit connection. Allowing the flow of energy to come together unified. I am now in the second limbo between the surgery, the drains being taken out, the vacation and then radiation treatments. I am always learning to practice patience. We all know the expression "God, grant me patience, and I want it right NOW". Be careful what you wish for because everything comes up that teaches us patience. I am patiently open to the intuition that guides me, especially when I remember to listen. We often forget that we are blessed with intuition and ignore the prickly forehead, or the gut feeling, when our Mind, Body and Spirit are saying something important. So I am working on turning up the intuition volume. I work very hard at being one with my Self. I am learning to listen more to what my body is telling me. It really works. I find so much peace in emptying it out of me onto the paper. It so helps to clarify the feelings and get them outside of the body. It is so essential for health and well being to breathe, to express the Self through the imagery. The honesty flows on to the paper and creates a vehicle to off load the stressors in a positive manner that, ultimately, is healing. Try it sometime. You will be amazed. Have a great day. Be safe, happy and true to your Self.

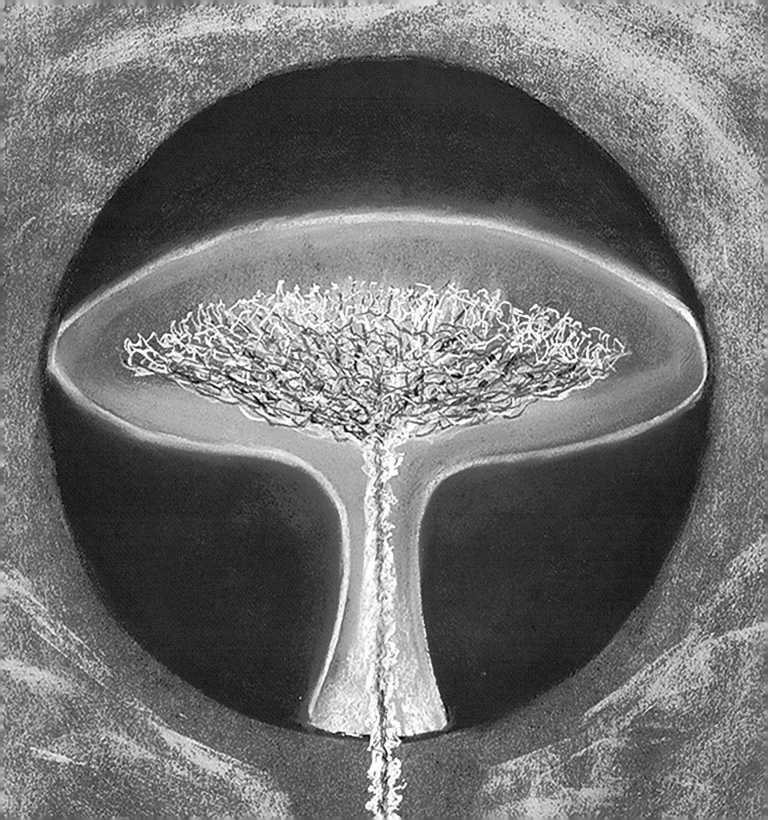

On the Journey: The Power of Healing Heart. Interesting, the Power we have in our mind, our bodies and our Spirit. I have been blessed with a drive for creative expression that sometimes even boggles me. I start out really tight and as I work each piece, I open up. I think that is how I am on the Journey, it started really tight and it is opening up for me, more and more each day. Today, I am in perfect health. As I have said before and will say repeatedly, I am cancer free. I am grateful for this Flow and wish you all a solid day. Having a new image everyday is, to me, remarkable and yet they come onto my paper. Seemingly effortlessly, they appear. I am always surprised. I want to share this passion. I will find a way. I encourage you to play with whatever media feels good to you: chalk or soft pastels, oil pastels, color markers, or water paints like tempera/poster paints; just scribble, doodle, move the energy you are feeling out on to the paper. It does not need to be a picture of something, that is your left-brain working and you want to be in your right brain. Whatever you create does not need to be perfect. It is the kinesthetic action that opens us up to possibilities of self-expression. I use the circle for containment. It is the metaphor for wholeness and that is part of my goal. Life opens up when we express ourselves. Enjoy. Play. We all have that beautiful inner child in us who loves to come out and play.

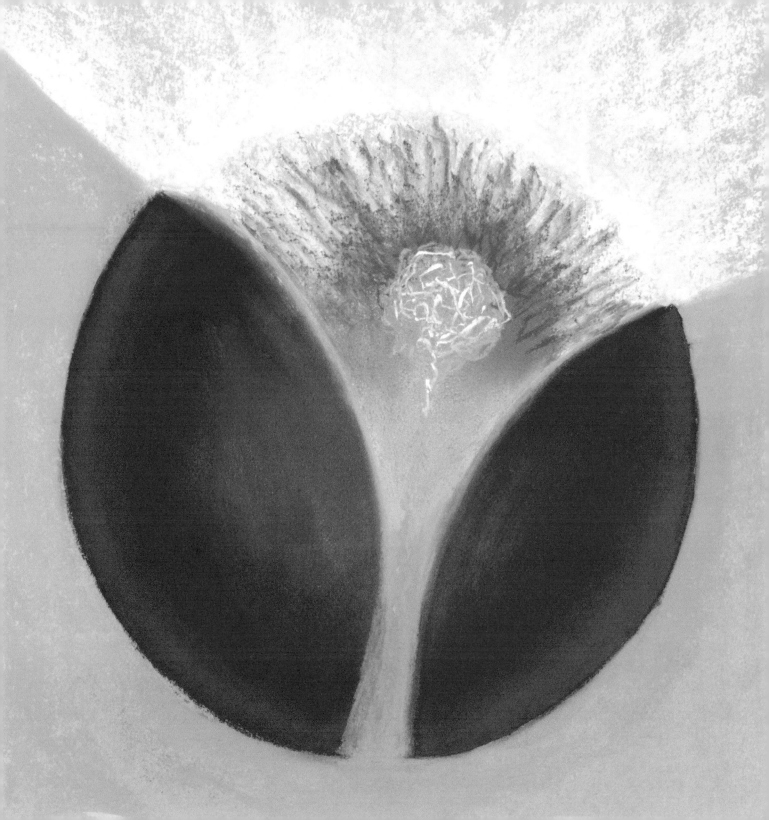

On the journey: The Power Beneath. When we go through this kind of ordeal, we are faced with hidden demons as well as strengths. We have to reach deep within our Self for the reservoir of strength through our Higher Power. The connection to Source bolsters our energy and our Spirit rises to meet the challenges we are facing each day. Cancer is a heavily laden word, but it is only a word. The definition, as per Webster's: 1. "Any of various malignant neoplasms that manifest invasiveness ... 2. A pernicious, spreading evil". So, immediately, the mind, poor thing, goes to death, which is the wrong way to go. I am in charge and we all have huge power on this path. We can stop the pernicious evil in our bodies from spreading. We can heal. I am healing. Modern medicine says drugs, drugs, drugs, without taking into consideration the best tool of all, US, our Self. This is the path I have chosen. My path may not be the best, and is certainly not for everyone. We have the wisdom in us to cut this pernicious evil out; purge it from our Mind, Body, and Spirit. This is my path. I listen, I learn. I am healing! I am empowered, free and looking forward to a vacation in southern Utah, far from the stress. Yesterday was the visit to the Medical Oncology Doc. I am cancer free at this time. They got it! The so-called "preventives" are not really sounding good to me; some of the side effects are congestive heart failure and/or possible anaphylactic shock. My heart already has issues, so I veto that one. More to the point, I am free of cancer at this time and have a 50% chance it will never come back, ever. I have discovered a fabulous community, which is here for me any time. I am so grateful. Each day I face the trials and tribulations of life, and I remember that I am not alone. I am in community every minute, whether I am aware of it or not. Being in the present is being at Peace. That is the goal. Here and Now. I am in the very best place I need to be, every moment. When we sit with that notion, life becomes amazing. So, present time is the peaceful place! Thank you all for being in my life and witnessing my Journey.

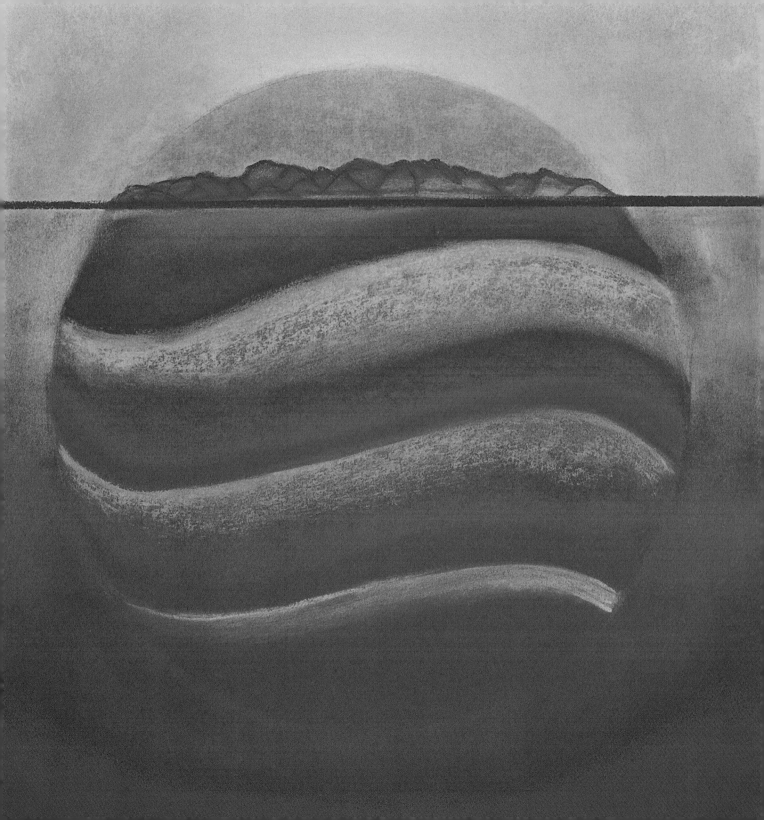

On the Journey: Energy Burst. We all have those moments when the energy just bursts out all over the place. We grow in leaps and bounds creatively, spiritually and it seems the energy does, too. Full of life, full of power and the creativity gushes forth. That is how this piece felt. Though it may have come out somewhat slowly for me, I had help; friends pointing out it needed something. Yes, we all, at times, have loving friends who are there for us, with encouraging words. It is then that the energy rises to the joint connection and, viola`; there is another on this path. I am blessed with new Angels at my Alter. A gift that warms my heart from a sister on this recovering path known as, (to borrow the term), "a thriver" from cancer. Everyday I learn something new on this Journey. First and foremost, that I am in the hearts of a huge community and that my studio is full of Angels basking me in healing energy every minute. This path is teaching me that humans can come together when one of their own is hurting. We have this amazing capacity for empathy and compassion. It takes my breath away. Gratitude is such an inadequate word, but it is in the language I speak. Yes, we all choose to thrive, not just survive. We are courageous and in a Sisterhood that is rich and deep, and full of loving acts of kindness and generosity. I am Grateful beyond words.

"If you are depressed, you are living in the past. If you are anxious, you are living in the future. If you are at peace, you are living in the present." Tao Te Ching by Lao Tzu: translation by Ralph Alan Dale, Watkins Publishing, London, 2002

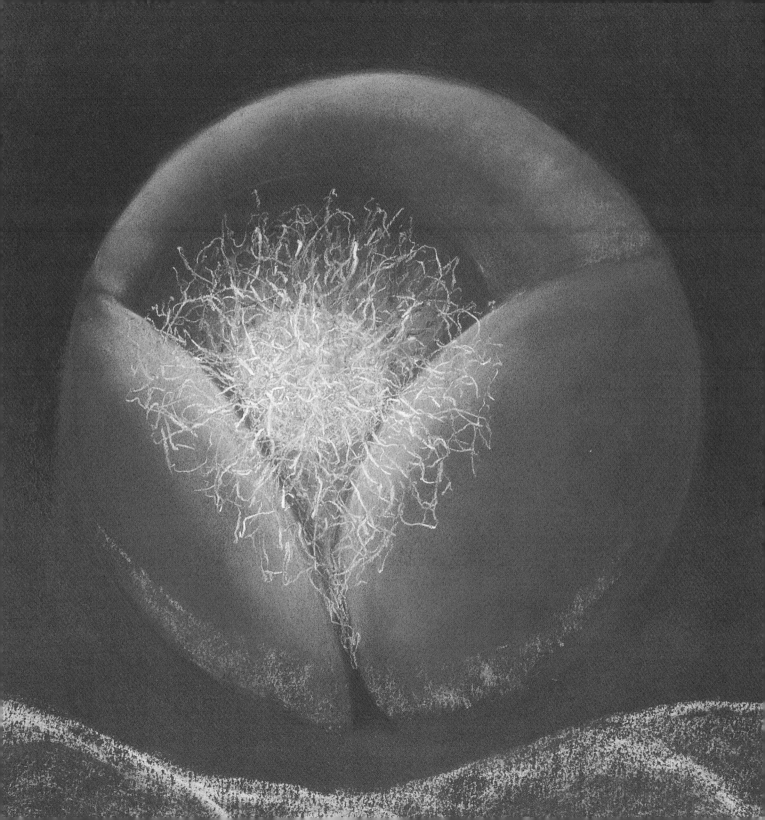

On the Journey: Another Kind of Holding. Good Morning World! Here is another day on this magical path. That is the experience I am having, many layers of emotions and feelings and moods. It can be very unsettling when some of the shifts are instantaneous. It sometimes makes life interesting. I stay in touch with where I am as much as possible. This Journey has had some little roller coasters but I am sure I am in for some world class ones. A friend asked me about the level of communication I was expressing. It seemed too reassuring, too good to be true. Well, in part there was truth in that. But I do feel good, I am confident I am on the right path. I do feel, to some degree, I am protective of those who may read On The Journey. So, The "BIG C" can be frightening for friends and loved ones to hear. It can change others' lives besides mine. I think I mentioned it before but I had cancer in 1980, successfully removed and no recurrence. I "died" in recovery because my body did not metabolize certain anesthetics. I stopped breathing and my heart stopped while the person who was supposed to be keeping tabs on me, went out to smoke or pee or to chat it up with a friend. I was on my way into the tunnel when, smack, I was back in my body. Wasn't my time yet. So, you see, I have a different view of cancer, as well as life. I have nothing to be afraid of, really. I do want the quality of my life to be at its best for however long I am here. I have no idea how the radiation will go other than good. I am cancer free as far as I or even the Doctors know at this point, so they say. This is the path. I am cancer free. I love you all because you are you, and I wish for each and every one of you, Joy, Every Day, however little or much. Enjoy, enliven, and embrace life NOW.

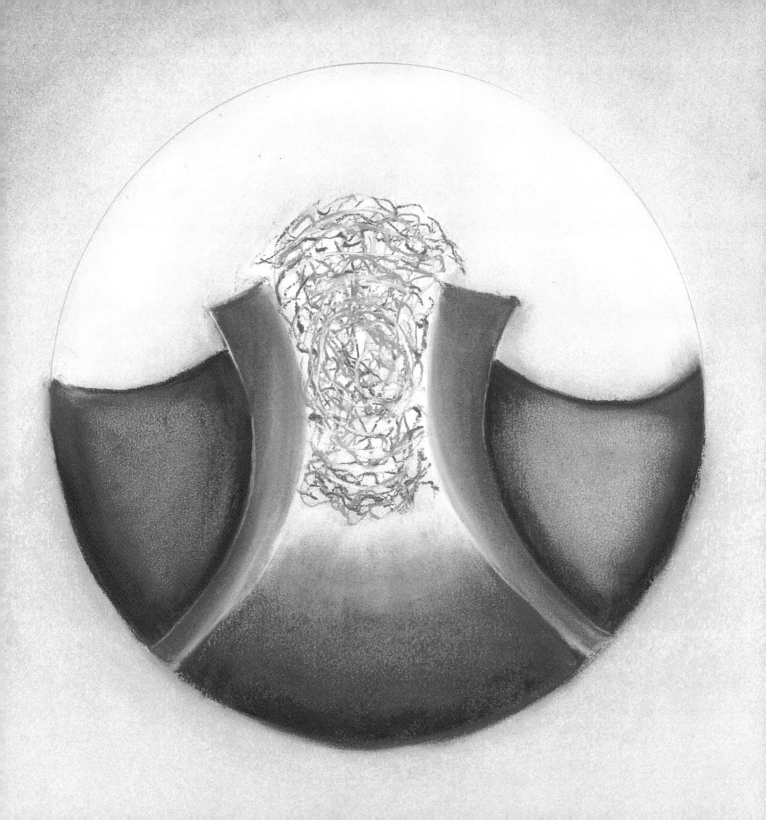

On the Journey: Segments. A new day on this path. Each day, as I present myself to the morning, I write, light incense, draw and meditate. I am ready for what the world has in store for me today. To settle me, I do a meditation that puts my feet back on the ground so I am able to finish the drawing. Thank you Robert Burns: "The best-laid schemes o' mice an' men gang aft agley". I love this quote. It is such a reminder to those of us who suffer control issues. So, the meditation today is to stay present so that every little accomplishment is a blessing and that tomorrow will be tomorrow. Can't change it. Today, I am here, present and full of energy. Sometimes, I am with a Presence who fills me with light and energy. Sometimes I am dim, not as connected. We are social creatures, who need touch, we need to look into each other's "I" and say, "I love you". Sometimes we just need to be there. Quiet. Present. There. We need to be open to Life, to the World, to Earth Mother, to our Higher Power and to the Great Spirit. We have that in us. Honor it, love yourself. Connect. So the thought of the day is: Living in the Now. Holding dear every moment until the next, and the next, and the next one comes along. Thank you for today! Things pop into my head, like the drawings. They just come, with the feeling of being held and supported by the Universe. Being in the present, the gift of Now. And again, thank you for today, Now. Enjoy Every single moment. Have a Glorious and Grand Day!

On the Journey: And Another Holding. I had the Radiology Oncologist appointment early today. 2 hours, 35 minutes later, we agreed to meet when I get back from my trip. The wound from the surgery will then be healed. I am over that hurdle. This Journey is full of hills and valleys, potholes, and then smooth as glass sailing. Today was a bit of the rough road of life. I had to also go back to the surgeon because the Oncologist did not like the look of the "wound". These Doctor visits are the most taxing because they seem to be there to help, yet are not, and are a bit cynical, callous and distant, all at the same time. I told the surgeon to call the oncologist. I finally got home to do the meditation and the drawing. I felt relieved, not so tired. A cup of tea is so restorative coupled with some self-expression. The down loading of the feelings helped me focus. It helps to put the crud on the paper so I don't have to carry it. I find it helps a lot to do the clearing. So enjoy, do some art, feel the relief, feel the paper, canvas, clay, whatever helps you feel the ah ha! Sit and feel the image in you, put it on the paper, the canvas or into clay, title it and write a sentence. Then put it away. That is how I work. Have a grand day, hug your loved ones and especially yourself. You deserve a good hug!

On the Journey: Super Structure: Good Morning World! A new day and a new direction. My trusty computer is full of glitches today. The hard drive is acting tired. So, the new one arrives soon. Life is such a blessing. The beautiful mountains to the south are snow capped, and yet still very inviting. They are reminders of the endurance of this great Earth Mother. Each new day brings changes, especially in the spring. More green, more flowers, and more hope this will be a better year. This year I will clean the 2nd bedroom so I can have company come visit. This year I will sort though all the "stuff" and have a garage sale. This year I will take a vacation with my sweetie to a beach somewhere sunny and warm. This year...... Well, I am here today. That is more the issue: Present, in the present. NOW. So, for today, I am here, now, present and alive. Through this process I am learning to be able to open up and trust me, trust the world and find some peace in my heart. I held in too much anger, hurt and resentment. When I got overwhelmed, I was done. I developed cancer. I need to do meditations of healing, living healthfully and being true to my Self, over and over. I am learning some of the phrases that really resonate for me. It has been a magical experience and I have to face some of the negative demons that still haunt some of the dark, deep recesses in my psyche. Today is a beautiful, count on your fingers, kind of day. The daffodils are glorious and even some tulips are in bloom. Weeds are burgeoning all over the place, too. In the middle of my drawing I had to pause, then finish the drawing later in the day. It morphed and shifted. I do not go there alone. Source, Great Spirit is always there to lift me and move me into creativity to resolve whatever is in my way. Everything in life is a lesson. Just like the cancer they cut out of me is a lesson. I need to let out my feelings and not hold them all in which I learned to do from a very young age. It is also a lesson to ask for help when you need it and not to always muscle through. So, I have a studio full of guiding, healing and joyous Angels who surround me, support me and guide me, when I listen. I am learning to do more of that, too! I hope you are all enjoying this marvelous day. Thank you for being you.

On the Journey: Downpour. I worked at the gallery all day, so I picked a drawing I hadn't shared. It must have been in anticipation of what was coming, on the Journey. I feel it reflects the feelings one goes through during a time like this. Overwhelmed with the support and surrounded by Angels, I do not feel the feelings as fiercely. But I do feel them. It is a strange blessing that I have been here before. May 8, 1980, I had been diagnosed with cancer of the cervix, had the surgery and "died" in recovery. I was resuscitated. I believe that is why I am doing so well emotionally, I know I have nothing to fear. I know I will be fine, regardless. God's Will. The idea of the downpour of feelings is true, regardless. Most of the time I feel very calm and accepting. It is Life and I embrace it as best I can everyday. I feel very secure on this Journey, that however it goes, I am doing the best for me and I will be fine. The Angels are telling me it is time to sleep. So, Good night, sweet dreams, sleep tight, don't let the bed bugs bite and if they do, pick up a shoe and beat the snot out of them. Enjoy every day; it is all we truly have when we open our eyes.

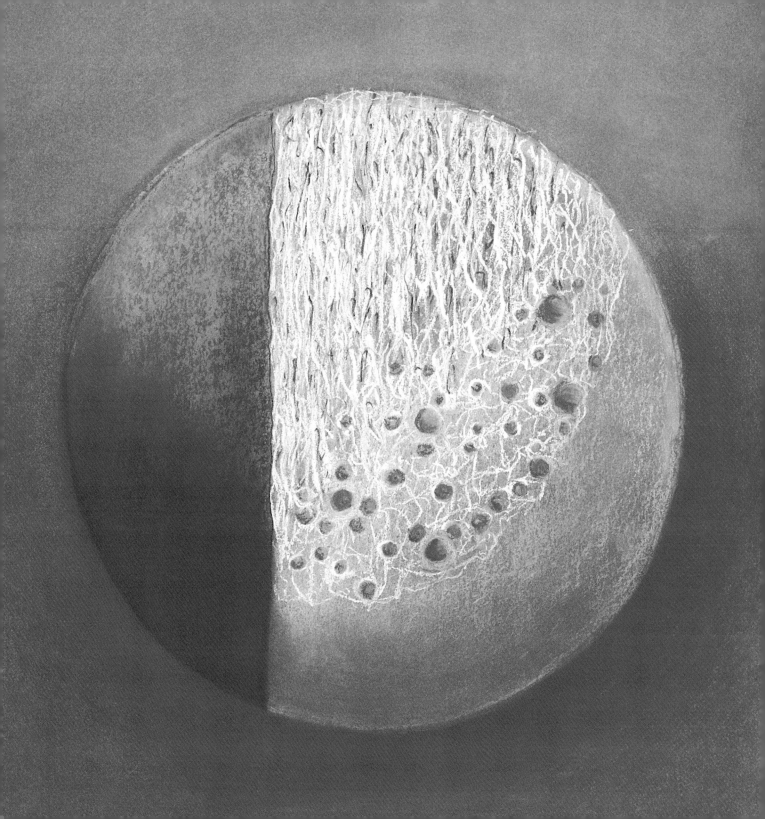

On the Journey: Twist of Fate. On this Journey there have been a number of twists of fate: the cancer, the surgeon firing me, the surgery, the recovery and the broken truck delaying my vacation. Regardless, this Journey has been a magical gift. And now the truck is in the shop for a mere $4,600.00+: new clutch, rear brakes and rotors and, and, and. Well, not all the and's. One of the few things I do not tolerate well is when people who are out right lying to me. Honesty is very important to me in my Recovery. I work at being true to my self. Honesty makes life very easy to live. One never has to cover their ass because they can't remember which lie they told who. My trip is delayed and I threw a little fit on the paper after I sweetly, politely pointed out to the shop supervisor that I really did not appreciate being lied to. So....., I decided that the Goddess has a mission for me to leave later than planned and that is what I am doing. The repairs took four extra days. So, I am practicing patience and kind thoughts. I embrace these twists and turns, usually after a moment of reflection. Life IS. I learn that every day. And there is so much for which to be grateful, as I have often said. In my journaling I close with a minimum of thanking God, Goddess, All That Is for Today! Sometimes it will be a paragraph of things, events and people that have come into my life. I have no idea until I open my eyes what the day is about. So, I am here, in the NOW. Healing and looking at the different options of treatment I have coming ahead of me. I will do what is best for me. Have a grand a glorious day. Thank you, All That Is, for today. And thank you for being here.

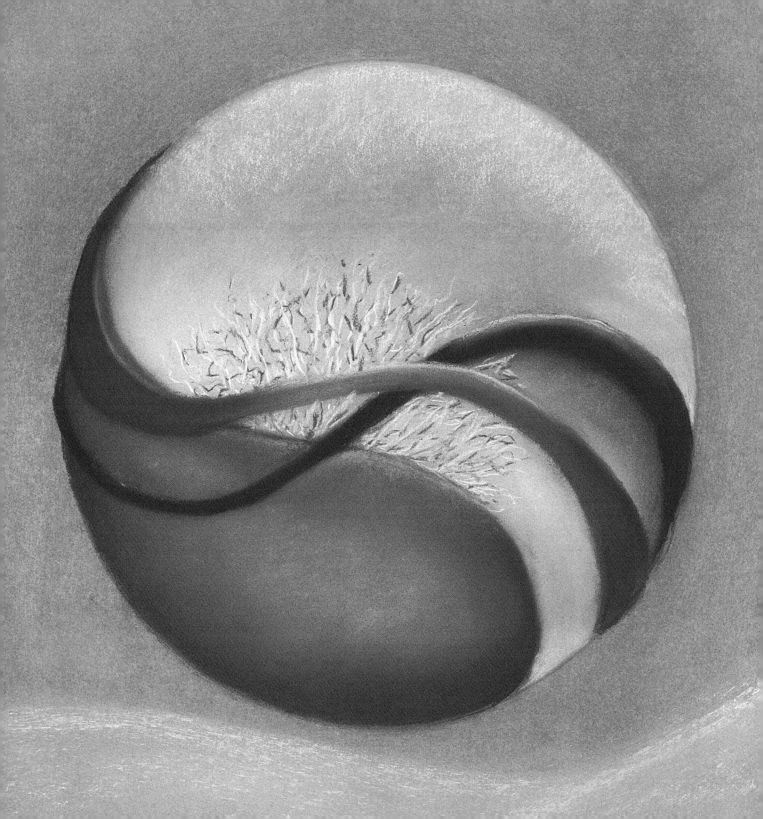

On the Journey: A Bubbling Healing. The Journey is going along. Today started out with rain and then it started breaking up. Then got cold and windy. We do need April showers for May flowers. I do look forward to some sunshine and 80 degree weather in southern Utah. The trip will be a little shorter because the truck broke. I will be heading out of here soon, singing "Here comes the Sun!" I feel very charged with energy and eager to be outside. I have been getting marvelous quotes from all sorts of sources. It is amazing where all this brilliance comes from. The power to share the positive is so helpful. There is so much out there to raise ones' spirits and make our hearts and souls sing. Some of the great poets knew how to "turn a phrase" in such a way as to open one's heart to the possibilities. "We honor ourselves when we honor the contributions of the spirit and creatively connect them to every aspect of our life." by Robert Piepenburg from Treasures of the Creative Spirit. This resonates with me and my philosophy of art and creativity coming through me. Each day with gratitude and prayer, I launch into doing a new expression of where I am in the moment, on this path. I find so much peace pouring this onto the paper. It is so helpful. It is so essential for my health and well being to breathe, and express my Self through the imagery. The honesty flows onto the paper and creates a vehicle to off-load the stressors in a positive manner that ultimately is healing. Try it sometime. You will be amazed. When we allow our "Self" to flow with the Spirit in our heart, magic happens. This is the best way I can describe what I experience, while I do my work. I feel all of us are blessed with an awareness that flows through us. It is a gift, and one only needs to be open to it. Thank you for the flow. I am ever so grateful for each and every one of you. Thank you.

I left for Southern Utah via Mendocino, CA to pick up my friend and fellow artist, Dana Driver. The trip was marvelous, but too short an adventure. We had mild weather then the rain, which follows me like a poor lost dog looking for what he needs. Then the poor lost dog turned into the trickster, in the form a coyote, bringing snow along with 26 to 30 degree lows. It did warm up again and overall the trip was great. We were off the grid for a lot of the trip. Did some art, took a mountain of pictures and visited breathtaking vistas. I feel much better.

On the Journey: Infusion of Wisdom. One day at a time. It is when we are reminded that Life Is, and we are Here, that we breathe in the magic and wonder of being here at all. We all can use a bit of wisdom. It comes when we least expect it, often when we most need it, and usually, if we are listening to our inner Source. Wisdom, when sought, is illusive but when we give up, sit on a rock, here it comes, right in front of us. I am always grateful for an infusion of wisdom that comes to me in the silence. In the space within me that is open. Wisdom is here and not, all at once. We lose it when we close our minds with "must, should, have to", and the like. So, for today I am in that special place, open to All That Is. Whatever comes, comes. Whether it is another challenge or a comfort, it is here now. I learn most when I am silent. I get the best gifts when I am silent. It is a place in me that fills with silence and overflows with love and gratitude. We become myopic, focused only on the stressor that is noisiest, in our face. We frequently forget to breathe. Stop! Take three deep breaths into your belly, and then exhale out from your toes. Feel the calm replace the tension, feel the easing of tight muscles, feel. I have to remind my Self to breathe. I have so many things that are shifting ever so much and slightly too, that I need to remember to pause, breathe, take in "where am I" right now? Breathe! For today I am infused in the quiet space in me. I am grateful I can find it and breathe it in, even if only for a few minutes. I found it and I am at peace. I hope you can find that silence that fills with love and gratitude with each breath.

On the Journey: Accent. Everyone has their own agenda. Mine is to maintain the quality of life I have, to the best of my ability. Some may think I have a twisted view in that I will not put any more poison in my body. I have done that enough. I did not treat my vessel well and I am paying now. Too bad we never listen to the wise words of others during the time we think we are invincible. I am paying the price with a bit of a funny ticker and cancer, a second time around. Having had a death experience; I have no fear of death. I do not want a drawn out horrid "illness" of dying either. I have made my peace with my Higher Power. I am looking at how I want to spend these last years, however many or few, as best I can. Family is becoming more important to me, friends more special and doing things that are meaningful. I love sharing the passion I have for art, for the creative process, for Art Therapy and the way art can give a person back their life. Participating in the arts is a lifetime gift that promotes self esteem, compassion, valuing each other, valuing life itself, empathy, discernment, communication, good judgment, perspective, perception, cultural values, respect for others' cultures, traditions and spirituality. The arts promote sharing, creative thinking, introspection, self respect, reflection and self-initiative. I want to share more of the passion with others, the way an art media flows and expresses the feeling the person is experiencing in the moment; the delight in small skills developed with a little practice and then the moment comes: There is a magic in the flow of a brush across the canvas, the sweep of supple pastel across the luscious paper, leaving trails of color where imagery explodes and the soul breathes, vital, alive, begging for the next stroke. This is how I feel and I want to share this more and more.

On the Journey: Gentle Encounter Within. I was fitted yesterday for what will hold me in place for the radiation treatments: 34 total. We sometimes put ourselves on a pedestal. It is so painful to fall off our own pedestal. I really love being human. I am perfectly human with all the flaws and foibles that go along with this species. I have been blessed with a modicum of talent and an overabundance of passion, determination and stubbornness. I do not imagine, for one moment, that everyone is as obsessed as I am in doing art everyday or following the discipline I demand of myself in my studio. The stubbornness and the demands I put on myself are not always very healthy. The way I hold my feelings in even though I am doing art work; the way I will practically die, literally, before I ask for help. I stuffed my feelings trying to avoid expressing them and look where it got me: cancer. I am changing the way I live to be healthier with better diet, more exercise, more meditations, more art, more honest expression of how I feel. I said that, didn't I? Living more in the present, loving and caring for me. Accepting who I am and being true to my Self makes me a better person to the outside world, too. I have looked at my Self honestly. I am not beating my Self up or being hard on my Self. I am expressing how it was, and has been. I am working on making changes in my life to treat me, my body, my Spirit and my mind with love, respect and healthy caring. Honesty with a hatchet is one thing, but clean honesty comes from a loving heart, which I do have. It is the gentleness that me, myself and I are encountering within all of me. Each day brings a deeper level of caring and understanding and love for all of me. Over the years I have been on many Journeys. Some journeys, I have no clue how they started, like the creative journey through the guidance/direction of Source, of the Metamorphosis Series: women/animal shape shifters. Each animal that came into my life brought healing/learning energies that I needed at that moment in time. Today, the mandalas are my teachers, bringing me insight, understanding and thoughtful contemplation. The blessings come on many levels. My job is to listen, be present and honor me, myself and I, and share my passion for art, creativity and Life. I share these things so others may learn to do their life differently! Have a Happy Day!

On the Journey: Blooming Insight. There are so many different levels of information, I sometimes get overwhelmed and have to pause, reflect, contemplate and breathe. I was reminded through some reading, how much meditation helps on these kinds of Journeys. I had started out with a meditation series, to be able to use the healing information to support this Journey. Then went off on my travels and lost track of it. I am back on. I do use it a bit differently but it seems to work for me. I sit through the meditation once. Then I go back to the beginning and while I am doing my morning Mandala, I listen again with headphones, so it really shuts out all the distractions. It has been a very powerful experience for me. I do this in conjunction with what the doctors are having me do with the treatments and the physical therapy. It is not a substitution for medical treatment. A Mindfulness Meditation practice is amazingly restorative and supports the mind/body/spirit system that We are. There have been numerous studies that have shown the benefits. The expression of where I am through the Mandala drawing is a form of meditation, bringing in the mindful meditation either guided by a master or by what I am drawing. Listening to Deepak Chopra, Wayne Dyer, Belleruth Naparstek or Angeles Arrien, as the meditation guides, can intensify the depth of meditation. Each person goes through their own personal Journey, whether it is recovery from an illness, recovery from addiction, or self-care to promote personal health in general. Each Journey is personal and can deepen one's faith in Life, in the Great Spirit and/or in God. Enjoy Every Day!

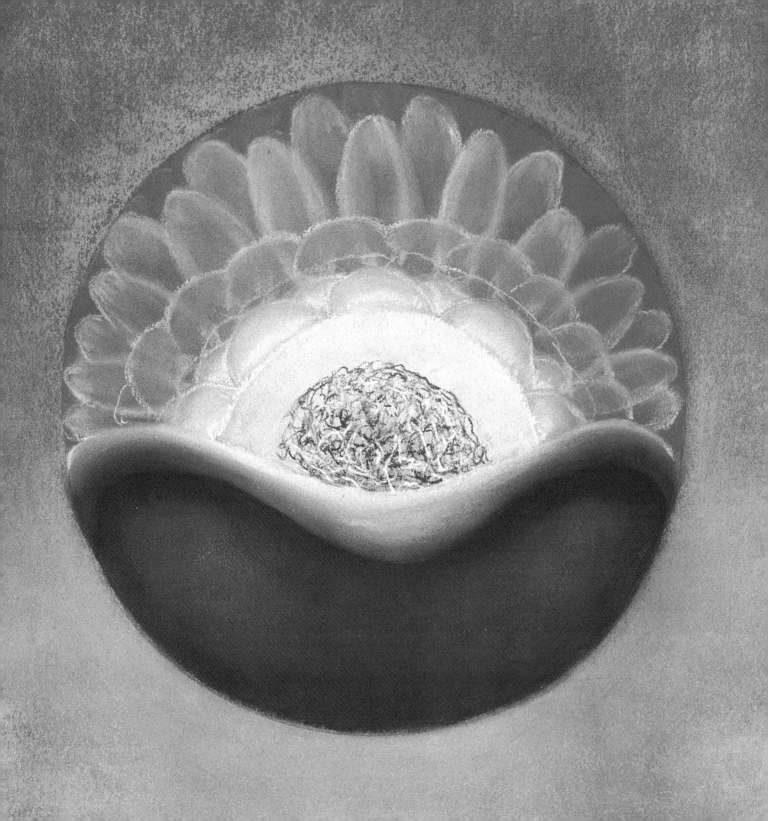

On the Journey: Engulfing. There is a light at the end of this tunnel. Each day I wake up eager to experience the new day. Eager to see where I am TODAY. Each day is such a blessing and full of surprises. George the cat, who thinks my worktable is his personal space, on my computer, on my writing journal, helping me write my morning pages, sprawling across my case of pastels that I have covered, he thinks for his benefit, just in time. Nudging for strokes, purring up a quiet storm. Life is a blessing of normalcy in my studio, which seems appropriate. It is a sunshiny day. Wow! We had the most marvelous rain yesterday, with amazing breaks of bright fresh scrubbed sunshine. It is a tad cooler today. I walked, with my neighbor, our customary three miles. She said I was walking at a better pace since I got back from my trip. Well, on my trip I was hiking at well over 6,000 and 7,000 feet. I do feel energized. Life Is and I am on board. I have always lived to eat and my chunky body attests to that. But walking helps. I find being outside, the fresh air, interesting conversation and a good pace is exhilarating and clears my head. Writing my daily 3 pages off-loads the garbage that tends to build up; my daily adventures within the circle all contribute to the balance and energy I need. Discipline, persistence, patience and practice are what keep me going on a level that is me. It is hard to explain, but self-determination for inner change can happen with self-discipline, persistence, patience, and lots of practice. It is hard to get a routine going that is different. Each of us can choose to help our Self, instead of doing everything for everyone else first and having no energy left for our own needs to be met. It is difficult to put your Self first. But the payoff is beyond belief and eventually others start seeing the benefits because we become a far better person. I do believe it rubs off, to some degree, on those around us. So, if you want more energy, create that little space in your day. I do my stuff as early as I can. By following The Artist's Way by Julia Cameron, meditate, walk, and write, you may experience the best sides of your Self. Play with art that works for you. And, of course, a daily dose of high quality chocolate helps, too. So life in the studio is as close to normal as it can be and it helps me on my Journey. Enjoy every day, waste none!

On the Journey: Some Meeting Elements: A grayish day though the sun has tried to come out a little. I am kind of going with the flow, with structure. My radiation treatments start day after tomorrow and go for seven weeks. I am not sure how to really express how I feel. I do feel like a kid on an adventure, mostly. Then the gruff adult says don't be ridiculous, this is serious stuff, radiation, how can you make light of all this? Then they banter back and forth in my head, until I finally scream STOP. They do listen. This is an adventure into a new experience I have never had before. I am keeping the quality of my life as best as possible. I am reducing stresses and changing my diet so I feel better. I am thinking about Yoga or T'ai Chi to get my balance in line again. This path is mine, what I have chosen. What is important is I have my friends and loved ones in my life. I do my art everyday. I talk to my friends, visit with them, go for hikes and walks, and do art. I share the passion I have for creativity, for healing with art. I feel blessed everyday. John and I went to the beach, hiked about and found a rock or two. It was a lovely day. Sometimes the sea, the sun, a breeze and good company make for a splendiferous day. It felt good to be outside in the fresh air. Walking about, taking a few pictures and just being. In fact it was a day for me. John pointed out how I have been very close to the chest (no pun intended) with sharing what is going on and about what was happening with the treatment path I have chosen. I did not quite realize how I was keeping information from him, partly because I was and am sorting through heaps of stuff in a variety of directions, and he never asked because he did not know what to ask. I think he did not want to hear some of it either. It is really scary for partners because they are watching from the sidelines and feel so helpless. What to do, what to ask? How to be supportive and be there for the person going through a challenging time? Also, I am a grand "minimitter". I made up the word years ago to help me, as well as John, understand how it can be difficult to express, entirely, what I am feeling when my life history was having my feelings discounted or disregarded. Even today I admit to feelings but minimize the admission. It is all about learning to trust those close to us when we feel particularly vulnerable. Old protective habits die-hard. Communications can help clear the air. Get out in the fresh air when you can.

On the Journey: Hold Still. I got stuck in the fitting/alignment for radiation treatment. The appointment was at 11:30 but they couldn't get it to line up by 12:30, and they had me come back at 3:00. I was in the treatment position until quarter to 7:00. I was exhausted from having to hold the cradled position for over three hours. There was some kind of glitch. I had six different people working on getting me all lined up. There was some kind of failure in the cradle form they had made last week that was giving them fits. I had to be still the whole time, other than breathing normally. The meditation practices I do were what saved me. I focused on a relaxation mantra, both visual and physical, from a past experience of snorkeling on the Kona Coast in the warm water with the brilliant colored fish and the sea turtles. Then I went into my mantra, working through my chakra energies. Time flew mostly. I would not have figured that I had been there over three hours in that one position. They were very kind, and very frustrated that the cradle was not working the way it should. They were also grateful I was so patient. I kept my cool and held the position. Acceptance for "what is" helped me stay calm and focused on being present holding the position. It finally worked. The treatment got done, and then for 34 more times over the next several weeks. Patience and acceptance of "what is" helped me through it. My body was glad to get out of the cradled position to go home and relax. Life is always full of lessons. I practiced mine: patience and acceptance. I am grateful for today. My plan is to keep my spirits up and that each day On the Journey, will bring new lessons to learn, free of cancer. The lessons are so varied. Today's was patience and acceptance. Other days, have been learning to open up to how I am really feeling, allowing myself to express the vulnerability I feel sometimes. Learning NOT to minimit my feelings. I am learning to be more present everyday on a whole new level. I always thought I was pretty present but I am learning to be more so. It feels more true to my Self, more real. Minimitting is a subterfuge. Honesty, being true to one's Self, is the lesson. Another one for the record, is learning to forgive my Self for hiding and minimizing how I really feel. This is the toughest lesson of all and I am still practicing. So, welcome to the Journey, we all are on one, of one kind or another. This one happens to have a huge healing component!!! Enjoy every day!!

On the Journey: A Transition of the Heart. I had to have the hard heart to heart with my Self about being straightforward and honest about how I am REALLY feeling, what I can actually handle without creating more stress. So, the best word for it is overwhelmed with information, appointments and responsibility of taking care of me. It is so much easier to take care of other people and ignore, be in denial, minimit our own feelings. So with that said, I am doing great. I just have to take care of me. So strange a notion, self-care; a very new concept for me. I have been a diehard co-dependent since I first could sit up. Taking care of everyone else's needs first and foremost. To put me first is so hard. This is the gift of being confronted with cancer. I can take care of me, NOW, in the NOW. I get to say "No! I need to take care of me first". The definition of selfishness is "the lack of consideration for the selfishness of others". Think on that. It takes a bit to wrap one's head around that thought, but it is true, too true. When we say "No", where we had always been compliant before, others get pissy because we are no longer catering to their selfish needs first. "No" is a very acceptable word. I am so grateful for the challenges and the lessons that come my way and this is a big one. This week has been a turning point for me in that I feel stronger and more capable of taking care of me on this Journey. I find that being open to these new experiences, feeling the anxiety about all the new "stuff", and then letting it go as I move forward has been the best direction. It is exciting and challenging; a total learning experience. As I said before, I am approaching all this as an innocent child with my eyes open, for the most part. All I can say is Thank you for your support.

On the Journey: Different Energy. I had a work....., work..., work..., get radiation treatment and never really paused until I fell into bed, kind of day. I took a short, 20-minute power nap in the midst of it all. Whew! I had hoped today would be better and, well, it was about the same but I insisted on doing art today. I was suffering horrible withdrawal symptoms: crabby, different than hungry crabby. Short tempered, impatient. None of these things are like me. So I did my art. I had an epiphany today about art. It is from one of those slogans: "Arts or Art Saves Lives." I then went to: "Doing Art Enriches Lives." Then "Supporting Art in Schools saves Our Civilization". So Spread the word, the support for arts in the schools is vastly more enriching, esteem building to all and is a gift of awareness of culture, our culture. OOPS! Sorry I got up on the soapbox. I just feel so strongly that a great deal of the demise of our culture is due to the lack of art, arts and creativity in schools from kindergarten through 12th grade. Oh well. It just had to come out. I am so grateful for the art in my life. Since childhood I have been an artist and it saved my life. It is enhancing my life On the Journey. So, go do some art. Just draw with any medium you like, using only line, form and color; it does not have to be of anything, only draw how you feel right now. Beyond The Artist's Way or Walking in this World by Julia Cameron, there are some marvelous books in which to participate. To name a few: Painting from the Source by Aviva Gold, Art is the Way of Knowing by Pat Allen, or either of the books by Michele Cassou: Life, Paint and Passion, or Point Zero: Creativity without Limits. Enjoy, play! I do.

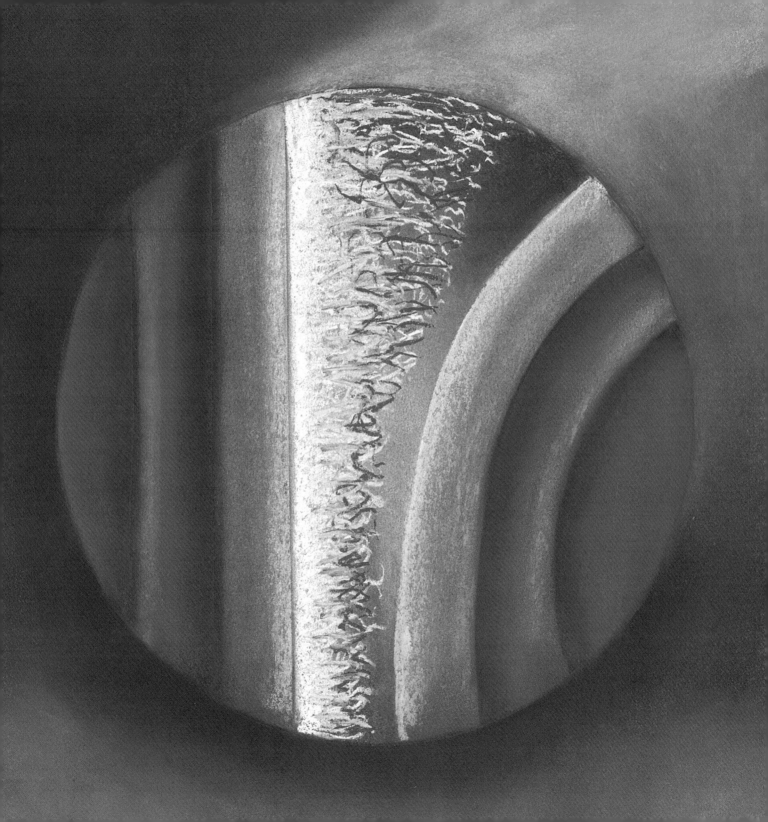

On the Journey: A Percolation! "That which does not kill us makes us stronger." Friedrich Nietzsche. So I am here! Doing art. Doing the radiation. Working at Gallery 9. Making Life happen. Life Is. I am here. After a few days in the lower mood frame of mind, I am back to my old/new Self. All the things going on in me, in my head, do have a way of percolating and then revealing themselves when they are ready or it is the right time. One learns to be quiet, let that quiet inner voice be heard. When we do pay attention to that quiet little voice, we learn great things. Sometimes it is just reminding us to take care of our Self. Sometimes we hear that we don't need to do something because in the long run it will not be good for us. Sometimes the quiet little voice shouts at us to shut up, be still and listen. Everyday I go for my radiation treatment. I lay in a "cradle" they formed around me in the position I must hold during the treatment. I found that this is a good quiet time, so I meditate and HOLD STILL. The great machine whirs, whistles and clicks, and moves on quiet gears and belts around me. It is the background noise for one of my daily meditations. I find it very calming, though this machine is "blasting" me with radiation to make sure that all the cancer is gone and stays gone. So, I take care of me while the machine does its' job! The purpose of the Journey is healing, sharing, observation and an ever growing awareness of human frailty and strength. This Journey is not just about me or for me. I am next to nothing, in the scheme of things, a mere drop in the ocean. Yes, the ocean is made up of gazillions of drops. I am one. My vibration spreads to those around me, to those around them, to those around them, ad infinitum. And I am still me. I share this because I know we are all on our own journeys, and that each journey is important, valid and meaningful. We do not live in a vacuum, we are all together. Some dwell in isolation and silence, for fear of being misunderstood, judged, ridiculed or.... heard. Some are silent because they think they have nothing to contribute. Well, we learn by listening, by being present, by engaging with our "fellow and fella" human beings. Life is and we are altogether on this rock spinning in space. Thank All That Is for Life. Sharing can be a gift, a different way of seeing what we never would have thought of without someone else sharing. I am so grateful for all the gifts on this Journey. Thank you. Enjoy Every Day!

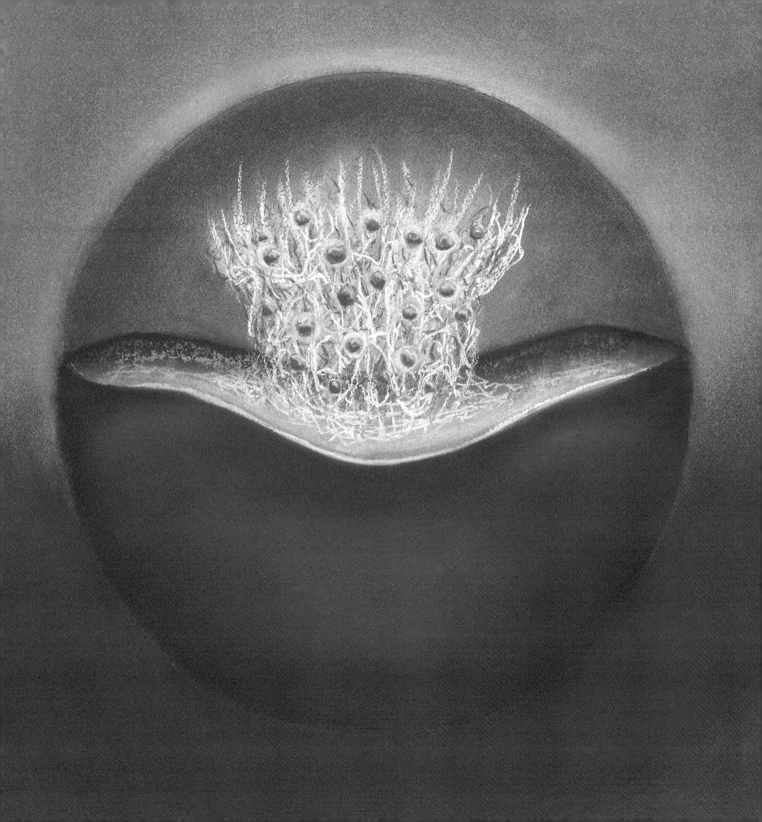

On the Journey: Held In. Happy, lazy, sleep-in sunny day! I was deep in a trashy novel, the plot had thickened and the bad guy was about to be royally busted. I could... not... put ... it down. I fell back asleep for a while. The guy got busted and I finally got my sorry butt out of bed at 11:08. I am not one to sleep in. I am the 5-6 AM, leap out of bed, scare the hell out of the devil, who gasps when my feet hit the floor: "Oh, shit, she's awake". It must be the radiation treatments, the supplements and the busy week.... time to slow down and relax. Relaxation, on occasion, is good for the soul. Also working in the dirt. I have three more plants to plant, a zillion dandelions to dig up and that is only one tiny bed. The dirt helps me connect with the Earth, grounding me in what is important. It all helps me be the best ME. Plenty of rest, good healthy food, exercise and art are the best things I can do for me. Working the soil is a reminder from whence I came. We all are made up of approximately 59 elements of the 118, all of which are part of the Earth. Every living creature including we humans, are made up of these Earth elements. The force of life makes these elements come together with energy with spirit with life. Breathe in the air. Michelangelo breathed this same air as did Geronimo, Leonardo Da Vinci, the Dalai Lama, Buddha, Christ, etc., to name a few. We are here now and in this Now, experiencing gratitude for all that we have: life, family, friends and loved ones. Gratitude for all the blessings, gifts, challenges and lessons we experience. Gratitude is another way to reel myself in when I lose my sense of being grounded. When I get caught up feeling down, depressed, like hiding away from the world or fed up with it all, I do a gratitude list. Gratitude for the air I breathe, for the water, clean running hot and cold water, the roof over my head and my ancient car, with gas in the tank. I list all the things I am grateful to have in my life. With each layer of gratitude I feel better. I feel enlivened. It is the fastest way to throw out the depression and re-engage in LIFE. It is a way to remind us we are blessed and we are alive. We have so much and we are safe. I am grateful for all who read this and contemplate on the Mandala. Maybe you, too, will be inspired to do more art, to write, to sing, to make music. Enjoy today, in gratitude.

On the Journey: Squashed. Don't know where that came from but sometimes the metaphor is hard to see, to experience and to take in. This one was easy. My spirit has been feeling a bit squashed by the treatments. The high-energy generator of yesterday is manifesting the level of energy that supports me without over-taxing me during the treatment. The squashed feeling had to come out and be addressed. I don't like feeling spent. I don't like admitting that I am tired. I don't like it when I am short tempered. I don't like running out of energy before the task is done, a task I used to be able to do without a thought. The "high" energy is in fact acceptance. Acceptance for where I am, Now, today. I am doing my best for this day. That is all I can do. My best is good enough. Ah, acceptance. We learn to accept where we are and when we are at peace in our Self. The sun is shining through the clouds and it is a great day! Sometimes I lose track of which day it is. The new time for my treatment is better, I can fill the whole morning and early afternoon with stuff. I will get the hang of all of this about the time the treatments are done. Anyway, I am finding that my fuse is shorter since I have not been resting well. Rest is the order of the days ahead. I am working on manifesting peaceful sleep, quiet naps and waking up feeling rested. The fatigue will be settling in from the radiation treatments soon enough. I am manifesting a higher level of energy that sustains the focus. Rest when I need to and Meditation helps me find that quiet place. All is well with the world when I am in that space. I see the sea turtles on the edge of the deep blue off the Kona Coast. I walk in tall golden summer oat grass that is soft to the touch and fills the air with a sweetness I have found nowhere else. In the calm space of meditation, the relaxation is deep, the mind settles to the quiet and the body feels like a feather in a gentle breeze, floating and light. When I come back to the here and now I feel rested and relaxed, open to new adventures. Rest, enjoy, play, nap, do art, meditate, and give and get lots of hugs.

On the Journey: An Embrace of Source. The sun is shining on this luscious warm day. Birds are singing. I am on my way to weed for a little bit before I have to go for a treatment. OK, it IS summer!!!!! At least for today. I saw a quote today on the Internet, with no credit. I cannot resist: "tomorrow (noun): a mythical land where 99% of all human productivity, motivation and achievement is stored." WOW! Isn't that so true, but we can change that for ourselves. We all have intentions and we put them off until tomorrow, where they live forever or at least a very long time. I like changing to manifesting in the now: I am doing art every day. I am happily eating only food that supports my health. I am energetically exercising every day. So you all get the drift: personal, present tense, and active participation in the now with whatever it is you want, NOW. We all know exactly what we don't want. This is where too much of our energy goes. But do you ever sit down and write a very specific list of what you DO want? Then apply the above formula of living it, NOW. See how good you feel? It is the first step toward manifesting what you really want. I am cancer free. Until they tell me differently, which they won't, I am cancer free. So, tomorrow is just a mystery, empty and never here. Today is where it is all happening. So, enjoy today, participate in what you want and be engaged in this summer day! Thank you all for being here, Now. You all are very special people. I heard from a dear friend about her sister's experience with a top notch Doctor when she asked him the best way to support her immune system: He said the best way is to rest and laugh. So that is the prescription to all of us in this crazy fast paced culture: Slow the flock down, rest, take naps, laugh, share laughter with friends and be Well. Like life, we are all so unique in our way of living and seeing the world. Life Is. We each approach it from where we are in the moment. This Journey has opened my eyes up to so much more. I literally see more around me. The colors are brighter, bolder, softer and just more intense. I feel the caress of a breeze rather than ignore the sensation. It is as if my senses were in sleep mode before and now are awake!!! The world is more present or, maybe, it is me, I am more present. I like being in this Now feeling. It is the awareness that each day is a gift, I am as full of energy as I can be during the radiation treatments. I am so grateful for what I have. Naps are on my agenda and my schedule now. I realize I am so lucky. I have made the choice for quality of life and mine is great. Naps help! Take a nap. Read a good book. Listen to music. Have a grand and glorious day.

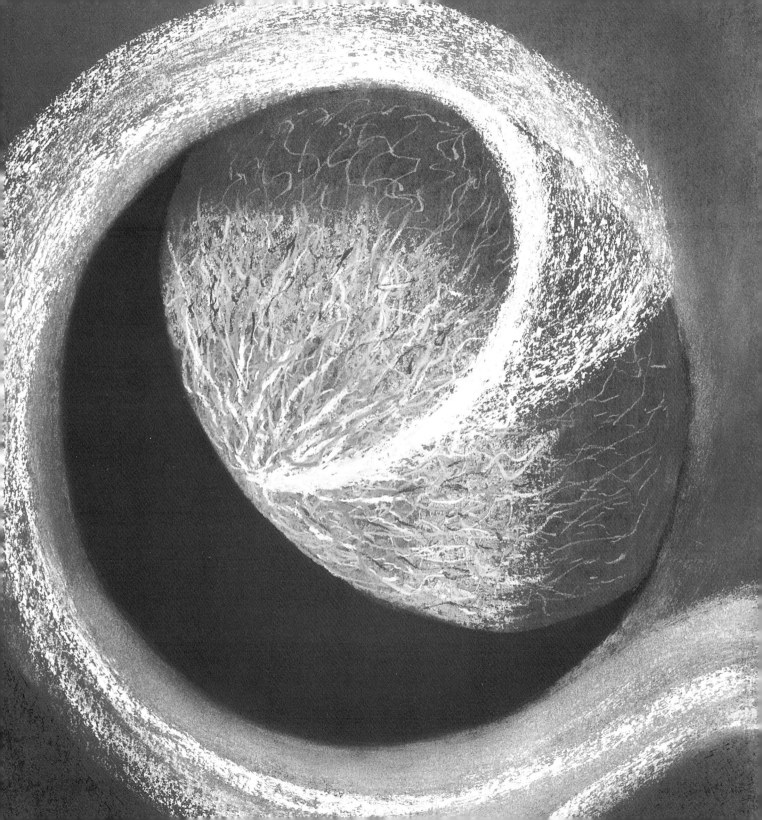

On the Journey: Deep Healing Energy. I have been thinking about this Journey on a lot of levels: the sharing, the catharsis, the inner journey and the art expression. Each person faces life's challenges in their own way. Some give up all their power to the doctors without question. Some research like crazy and choose to follow the hard line statistics. Some travel their road in fear of dying. Some travel their road with their eyes wide open. You know I am traveling my road, pretty openly. I did a fair amount of research. I have spoken to some survivors, thrivers and sisters on this Journey. I have said it before: my choices are based on the quality of my life. I chose to take the most direct, least disrupting path, not necessarily the least invasive. It is a path that suits me. Art, the expression of where I am in the moment, heals my soul and my body. Life Is and I am here. Nearly 24 years ago I made a huge shift in my life. I quit drinking. I joined the 12-step program, went into therapy. I worked with both a psychologist and a body worker who was a kinesiologist. I went to meetings. The things that were locked in my body were released and the shrink facilitated my mental recovery of my past and the reasons for self-medicating with alcohol. I lost everything that was my life's foundation and I had to start over, rebuilding a new foundation and a new persona. It was a journey where I had to fight for my life to rebuild it. This current Journey is very different and the same all at once. AND Art, the emotional expression of where I am, saved my life then and has done the same now. Thank you for sharing your thoughts with me, your love, and your support. I am grateful beyond words. Enjoy everyday!

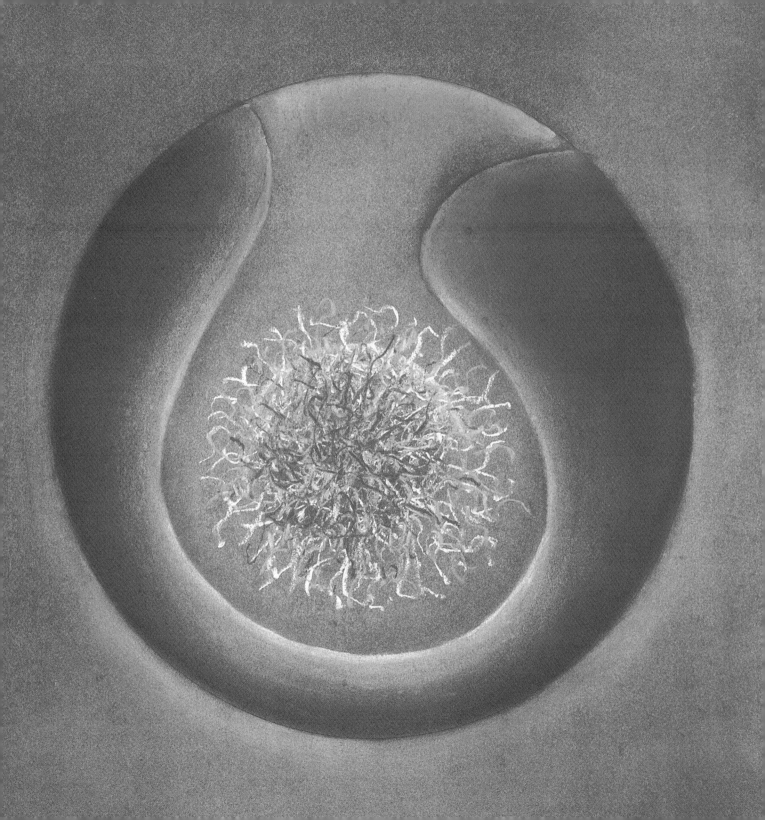

On the Journey: Caught in the Trap. Today I get to go in early for Re-calibration of the beam. It makes for a longer session. It means we are focusing in on the most affected area and then in 19 more treatments I am a free woman again. I am so very impatient to get to MY life without treatments and doctors. They are all good people; I just want them out of my life for a long, long time. The cancer is gone and life goes to the new normal for me. Like the Amazon Warrior, to shoot her arrow straighter she cut off her right breast. It was always my dream to be tall and strong like the Amazons I read about in mythology as a young girl. I stopped growing at 5'4". Not the Amazon, but strong and full of determination. I still have it! I am planning on doing more art, more shows, this book and traveling a bit. And more adventures to come. No time like the present to be present. I bring the light into my work. I felt somewhat lighter today. The new simulation measurements were done. Got a 5th tattoo. Guess I need to get a really pretty one to cover the dots that sprinkle my right chest area once this is all done. The surgeon is going to re-evaluate the scar later. I did not heal well. Looks like an old gunnysack stitch job with the string pulled too tight. Not a pretty picture. Ah, Vanity. So many things to think about that are really more important than vanity. The list is long and varied. Thinking about getting back on the show circuit to sell my work. I am thinking that I do so few bronzes, showing the 2D work is more manageable. The new work has me really quite engaged. There are always the mixed media pieces that are screaming: do me, do me, do me, NOW! It is always amazing when the energy flows openly, how active the creative juices flow. It is that first step, that first commitment to doing work on a daily basis and following through. The flow may start out slow, be persistent, patient and practice every day. The flow comes with determination. "Can't" just isn't in my vocabulary when it comes to my artwork. So, I share this to encourage others to do what you love, it will flow when you persist. There was a nice write up about six very talented, passionate women artists in <u>Living on the Peninsula</u>, recently: Dee Green: a ceramicist, Susan Martin Spar: a painter, Martha Collins: a wood worker, Pat Oden: a quilt maker, Inge Norgaard: a fiber artist. And about me, doing my eclectic work. Wow! A great issue, great talent, and great stories. Inspirations to others. There are a lot of talented and passionate women artists out there. Do art, write, and make music. Nap, play, walk and enjoy nice weather. We are all blessed.

On the Journey: Resting. I watched a good movie: <u>The Life of Pi</u>. A journey of great courage, whichever story was true for Pi. It seemed to reflect the depth of our determination, as humans, to survive. The power of the act of surrender to our Higher Power, which gives us the strength to go on. The story really moved me. When we have life threatening illnesses, like cancer, we choose our path. One of determination and resolve to be well, to participate in the wellness is the one I feel I am living. There are many ways to face the threat and we can choose to see it as an opportunity. The lessons we choose to learn from our experiences on our path can bring us enormous peace. We choose. There are occasions when the battle is over, yet the lessons still need to be learned. We transition to the Great Unknown, with peace and love in our hearts. Whatever course we take, it is the right course for us, only us. Finding peace in our heart of hearts is expressed through the way we choose to live in the Now, present, positive, active and alive. It seems I am in a philosophical mood. This bump in the road is a gift that has brought me, to this point, a great deal of peace. It is proving to be a Journey as much for healing my Self as my body. I feel alive, awake and determined, as a participant, Healing everyday. Letting go of the trivial, embracing what is important, to the best of my ability. I think it will be nice to go weed. Weeding is a good metaphor for letting go of "things" that are not assets to our inner garden. We all struggle while hanging on to attachments that do us no good. The quote I use is "Attachment is self imposed suffering". We do that. Weeding out the things that no longer serve us is a good idea. Think of that dandelion, right in the middle of your beautiful flowerbed. It is time to dig it out because if it is not dug it out it will come back tenfold. I am off to weeding in the nice weather, then treatment and then rest. Enjoy this great day. Play, enjoy and laugh.

On the Journey: Bubbling Inspiration. Bubbling ideas and thoughts that seemingly arise from the depths of Source inspire me to do the work everyday. It is interesting because frequently I feel I need to keep up with all the ideas, then I know I can do any of them, whenever. I do not have to do them all at once. I have been through dry spells. They are painful and crippling. My method to bust through the block is to write, to push, to do projects from books. A great example of a block-buster is <u>The Beginner's Guide to Constructing the Universe: from 0 to 10: The Mathematical Archetype of Nature, Art, and Science</u>, by Michael Schneider, 1995. The adventure through the numbers was so remarkable and the projects that one could build, like the dodecahedron, tetrahedron, octahedron and an icosahedron. These volumetric structures are fun to construct. Doing these projects helps one, literally, get over themselves, get out of their own way and back into the flow. When I feel blocked, I re-evaluate my philosophy. I would like to share it. I really had to think about what is my Philosophy about why I do art. It is fairly simple. Using Webster's definition of Philosophy: "b. inquiry into laws and causes underlying [my] reality". The laws and causes of MY reality are: I do art. I live art. I live to do art. Without the artwork, I feel I would shrivel up and blow away. Then again when I shrivel up and I am about to blow away, there will no longer be my work. Without art, what are we anyway? The creative process is what drives me. I have worked in a lot of different mediums and find they all fulfill something in me, each differently, but each journey has brought me closer to my true Self and the Source of the creativity. Isn't that the goal for which all artists are striving? This is part of examining what drives me to do art and the work I do. Where the determination is born. Sometimes it is a challenge to be able to even get up, to stand before the easel and "see" the color that is the beginning. But I am here and the color comes and the work has begun. I trust that beginning color. It takes away the fear of the empty page: white, blank, stark and bare. Play is what it was and is all about. Don't take it so seriously, enjoy, get it? En - joy; fill your Self with joy. This is what has worked for me. Have fun. Play, scribble and express where you are at this moment.

On the Journey: Bubbles of Energy. Are we here by accident? Our question: why are we? What made us happen? What moves us to exist? What gives us joy? These are all such esoteric questions. Where is my head today??? I worked hard yesterday at Gallery 9. Had a lot of really nice sales! Made a number of fellow artists happy. Came home exhausted. The radiation does dampen my energy quite a bit more than I would like to admit. I don't have too many more treatments, then I want to take a vacation. Hopefully my energy level will start improving soon. So, back to my weird, normal, crazy human questions. Why are we? Life in itself is a question, then compounding it with "intelligence" and the ability to ask WHY. A deer does not question its existence. It lives, eats, sleeps, runs for its life when its life is threatened by another creature; a lion does not question its role in the balance of nature; it is just hungry and there is dinner on the hoof. But we ask why, why are we here? We must connect, we need to belong, we feel emotions and we desire useless objects that clutter our homes. Can you see a critter tricking-out its den with objects? Only ravens, crows, bowerbirds and pack rats collect "junk". Ah, the funny meanderings of the mind. "Why" is an auspicious question that cannot be answered adequately, yet we strive to reach that level of consciousness, only to realize: what difference does it really make why we are here? We Are. Acceptance is the path to peace of mind. Living in the present, awake, aware. I have so many art projects that I want to get to but that energy just isn't always there. Doing the pastel drawings fulfills creative drive to some degree. Doing art on a daily basis has kept my spirits up because I move the energy out, good or bad, easy or difficult, it makes no never mind, as they say. I just present my Self to the paper with the colors at hand after I do my morning writing, meditation, and prayers. What comes is where I am. Sometimes the title is the worst struggle. It is not always easy to express in words how I am feeling. It is just there. It means a great deal to me to share this journey, so that others might learn and find a path that fits them by doing a creative and expressive piece daily. Sure, I have missed a few days here and there, but not many. If it is helpful to anyone, I would be happy to answer any questions on how to get started, to get over the obstructions, distractions and the wet blankets that get in the way of our creative process. So, do art, play, laugh, nap, walk and enjoy your day!

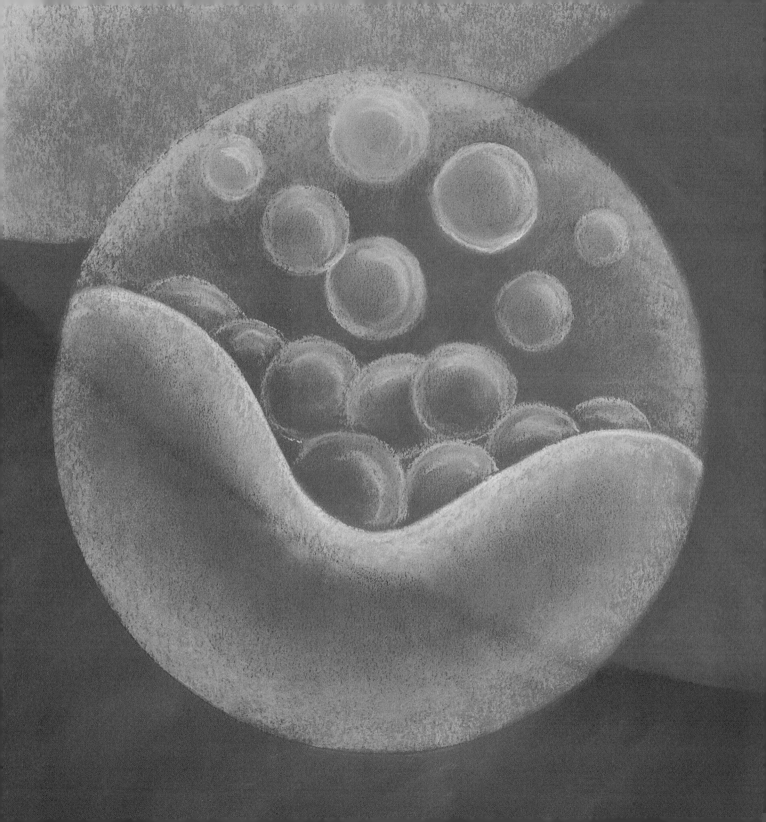

On the Journey: Caught in the Flow. I enjoyed the morning sun, looks to be a glorious day. It is a great day to be out and about, in the sun and enjoying the day. So, enjoy some, too. I am. I started the day off with this very fast drawing. I had this in mind, the little bud being held in the dynamics of the vortex. The Flow that swirls and is seductive. That is the driving force for my work. It is captivating to do art everyday, nothing else matters but the expression that flows onto the paper. To be driven like this is a mixed blessing. I feel a sense of purpose, of moving the energy and sharing the expression of how I am today. It is healing. There are things that I have not been taking care of as well as I might. Finding balance in one's life is always a challenge. I see my time, each day, gets delegated to the drawing, to food, to the treatment, to post treatment care, to resting, to engaging with other people, to taking care of the critters, to worrying about John and what is happening with him. This leaves a few minutes to breathe, to pause, to reflect and to go to that quiet place. The house is the last thing I think of. Something I will get to in the next pause in the whirlwind of my life. It is important to me to be aware of the delight of being a flawed human, being human completely. In the here and Now, I know I am not alone on this Journey and I am ever so grateful to all for the support and love that surrounds me. Thank you for being human, too.

On the Journey: A Burgeoning Health. Yes, I have been on an adventure that is reminding me of things I need to remember: Self Care, Letting go, Forgiveness of others, and especially Forgiveness of myself. Being true to my Self and, as always, the Gratitude for Now. Each day has revealed new things that are seemingly so simple yet baffle me to do them regularly: telling someone we care, making a meal for a friend who is sick, giving someone a ride when they can't drive, listening (now that is a big one). Just listening, letting another person have a witness to where they are, what they are going through. Not trying to fix it or change their mind or insert your opinion or discount what they are feeling or where they are in this moment. It is so important for us to be quiet, at times, and hear, truly hear, what another is saying. Sometimes I do it really well and sometimes I fail miserably, but I do work at listening. In my practice as an Art Therapist, I do pretty well, most of the time. It is my Job to listen, to be a witness to my client's path. The Mantra that I work at using is from Angeles Arrein's Book: The Four Fold Way: Show up; Pay attention; Tell the truth without blame or judgment; Do not be attached to the outcome. The show up and pay attention parts are essential to listening. Then if they ask for advice, help or your opinion you go to the next: tell the truth, your truth, without blame or judgment. The kicker is "do NOT be attached to the outcome". Seems really simple, right? Wrong! It is something that one must practice and practice and practice. Listening is an honor. The speaker is asking of you to just listen. Ask simple questions when you must, but just listen! It is a gift to learn. Enjoy your day.

On the Journey: Visions. This is the first of a series of Visions; images that float through my mind's eye while I meditate during the treatments. They pulse through and captivate my attention, soothing, graceful, and inviting. This is a relaxing feeling that allows me to float through the treatments in a somewhat contorted position. Yes, the fatigue level is increasing and self-care is the only way to deal with it. NAPS. It is a really profound lesson in how stubborn one can be about change. Damn, it is hard to power through stuff on dead batteries. Self care, relax, take naps, laugh, nap and relax and nap. I find this to be important. Life Is, and I am here, doing the best I can for me. I am glad I can meditate through the treatments. The core of me is really solid, but sometimes I feel a little cracked around the edges. Vulnerability is hard for me to warm up to. I sure as hell don't want anyone to think I am needy or weak. Heaven forbid, me, show my frailties. HA HA HA! Isn't that the truth, we all like to try to be a better person than we think we are. This IS the issue. We think we are less by showing any "real-ness", as if it is a sign of weakness. Somewhere in the writings of Buddha is a story about the Poppy. I heard a sermon about the Poppy being the best Poppy it could be, that a Poppy has no aspirations to be a rose or a dog, or anything other than what it is, a Poppy. Why is it we, as humans, are so stuck on not being good enough, not being happy with who we are? Just us, the best "us" we are. Here, now, at this moment. It is a struggle many face, not accepting one's Self for the kind, caring, hard working, contentious, beautiful person we are. I know the struggles I go through accepting me for me, for who I am, in this moment. Sometimes it is difficult to see my assets, yet I can see them in others in a moment. We don't give our Self credit. I look in the mirror and see a great person there, with all the flaws and foibles. I am still a great person, and it is I. We are harsher on ourselves than on others. We look for and see the best in others when we cannot seem to find it in our Self. I work at being the happy Poppy. Be the best; honor your Self as the best person you are NOW. Today I celebrate Life. Every day is sacred. Every day holds magic and joy. Every day I choose life for today. Naps are good and Chocolate warms the Soul.

On the Journey: Visions # 3. Like waves flowing over my mind, body and spirit, the energy sweeps me back and forth: from feeling empowered to utter exhaustion. The kind of fatigue I have is somewhat unrelenting. My body is working hard to cope with the bombardment of the radiation, which is the origin of my fatigue. Having additional stress components just did me in: we spent another night in the E.R., John has been passing kidney stones. So, the waves of energy are in the depleting mode. Rest will come after my treatment today! I work hard to maintain a semblance of normalcy, but the batteries are depleted. Whatever second wind I might have had, has long since blown away. It is time for more than naps. It is time to rest, take a day off and sleep, without interruption, as long as I want. Right. My silly mind thinks this is nothing, just another bump in the road. We can handle anything. Well, sweetie, let me tell you something: listen to your body, forget the mind and rest. The energy will be there again after some rest. I have only a few more treatments. Whew!?! Be smart, listen to what your body needs and indulge in the decadence of sleeping late, in a comfortable bed, quiet books, major reduction in external stresses and yes, a little chocolate everyday! The silly, sad, magical thinking, vestiges of childhood, which makes us think we are invincible, just have to be confronted. I am very vulnerable, I am not invincible. Trying to function on dead batteries just doesn't work. This is part of how the cancer gets a foothold on our body; we do not have the "energy". We do not have enough Natural Killer Cells to destroy the cancer naturally. We have allowed our bodies to be so depleted of energy through poor diet, chronic low-grade malnutrition because of poor farming practices; not resting, really resting; environmental stresses and pollution. All of these factors contribute to zapping our reserves of Natural Killer Cells. I have the power to turn a new leaf and take care of me. So do you: reduce stressors on your life, laugh a lot, good food, nap when you need it and of course a little dark chocolate goes a long way. Enjoy every day!

On the Journey: Heart Source. For today, I am resting. One of the gifts of the Journey is that I am looking closer and closer at how I want to "spend" my time and energy. What kinds of things are really important? Who is a wet blanket or crazy maker in my life? How can I make the best use of my time? What IS really important? What or who is sucking my energy? What feeds my Soul? Examining just these few things in my life can make a huge difference. Sometimes those around us don't want us to change. It upsets them because we are not predictable any more. They think we are being selfish. A definition of Selfish: the lack of consideration of the selfishness of others. Think on that. Twists your head a bit. The focus on Now really affects my choices in what I want to do, Now, at this moment. Sure there are things that are in the future, but Now is what I have for sure. Colors are brighter, the flowers smell better, food tastes better and I only eat what I want to eat. If I don't like it I don't eat it anymore. No clean plate rule! These are just a few things I have noticed. I have the determination to work on getting my artwork out and promoting it. I see the need to re-engage in the showing and marketing of my artwork. Life is full. The shadow has receded a bit, though still ever present. I am here Now, present and enjoying the time to reflect. Mercury went into retrograde, so it is truly a time for deep reflection, assessing projects, contemplation of future plans and ideas, and looking at projects that might be fun to do when life goes direct again in a couple of weeks. Some projects I may let go of, as they really are not important. So enjoy the day, smell the roses, eat that luscious peach and breathe. Watch the subtle shifts of colors in the clouds. I am grateful for all the loving support, prayers and Angels that are sent by all you beautiful people. Wander about in the garden. Nap, play, enjoy, today!

On the Journey: A Kind of Grace. This is a relief from the visions for a while. In contemplation, I am pulling a lot of little projects together in my head. Some projects REALLY need to be discarded, some I REALLY need to get to work on. With Mercury in Retrograde it is a time for reflection, contemplation and introspection. Do I really want to go down THAT road? Yes! This is the path that inspires me, gets my juices flowing to create more, to dig deeper, to look inside and seek out the debris that needs to be cleared out. Put the debris out on paper to move it out of my body. The path is clean and clear. Determination and discipline to move forward are really most important. Patience, persistence and practice are the path that works for me. "Don't quit!" is my motto. Don't give up. Keep working at whatever moves you. I read a study recently about stress reduction in the American Art Therapy Journal. Active creativity i.e.: doing art, over passive activity, i.e. observing art reduces stress. Art materials are tools for healing. The other newest and best addition is to title the piece, then write a short sentence or paragraph about it. By doing the art, titling it and explaining the art, that act moves energy out of the nonverbal right brain to the verbal left brain, then the two halves develop a path to communicate, to translate the image into an explanation in words. These are very important components that can heal so much, helping so much and changing thinking patterns in really healthy ways. Just thinking or just talking about the "expression" of a feeling is not enough. By expressing our feelings using the art process, regardless of the material, joined with verbalizing the feelings expressed in the art, translates the expression and opens a door into the inner communications on whole new levels in the brain. Play, enjoy, and express your feelings on paper, in clay, with paints. Title it. Laugh, cry, and do more art.

On the Journey: Vessels. I find it interesting that I need to work within a circle, and then I draw vessels, just another form of containment. Seems that the working metaphor for me is, in fact, containment. It is just plain terminal, but so is life. Many so often live life in fear and denial of the eventuality of Death. Death is part of life and really is the incentive to live the very best life we can, NOW. Life is like a painting. We can fully engage in it or we can stare forever at the blank canvas in fear of not getting "it" right. We can dive in making a mess of it and salvage it with heroic measures, ending up with a masterpiece at the proverbial pearly gates. WE choose how WE live. I believe Albert Camus had a philosophy that I will try to paraphrase: One has a choice when waking up in the morning: of committing suicide OR having a Great day. I choose to have a great day. I can choose to embrace life. Paint like there is no tomorrow and get up the next day and do it again and again and again, one day at a time. The vessels hold the Source of creativity that is in everyone. We only need to reach in and get what we need, from our heart. Enjoy a great day, however it is, today. This can be a beach day, a walk in the mountains day or just a walk outside in the air kind of day. One of those "Lemonade from real lemons" kind of days. Have fun, you deserve it.

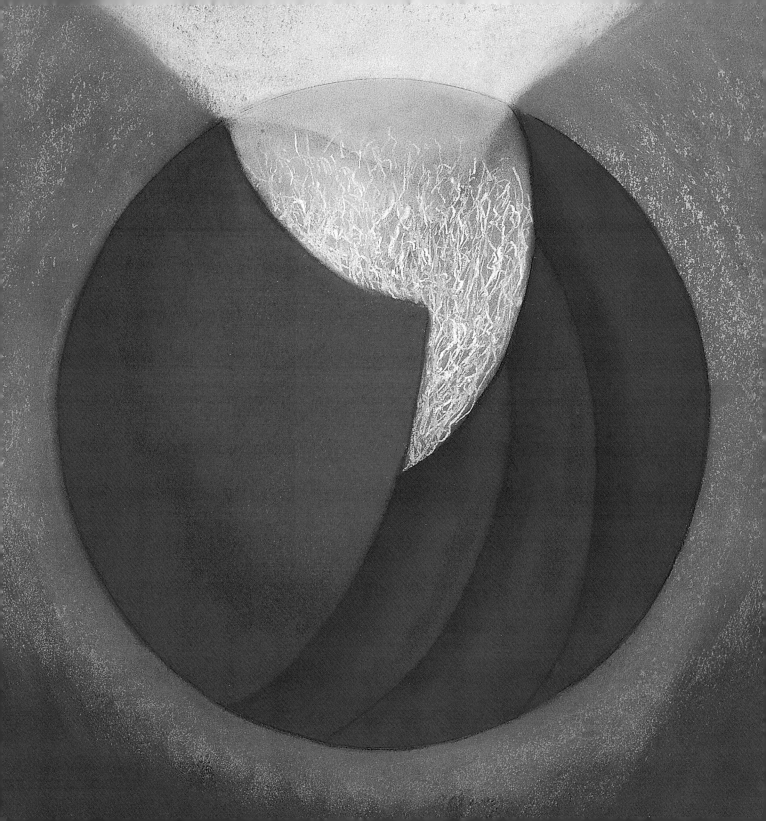

On the Journey: Zapped. I do take a few cat naps while doing the saline compresses, I just nod off for a little while. It is good to do. I have some extra tasks to take care of with John still very much under the weather. Today, I had to bury Gertrude, the turkey. After having her for over 4 years, her cumbersome weight got the best of her as she had lost the ability to walk at all which brought on other health issues for the 60 + pound turkey. I am glad she has transitioned to her new life. Maybe she will be a songbird or an eagle in her next life. I have always prayed for the chickens before I butchered them that they might come back in their next life as a graceful heron or a soaring eagle. I want them not to have the life of a meat bird again. I wish the same for Gertrude. It is a Buddhist belief that we transition from this life we have today to a different level, depending on our Karma. When the end comes to this physical form, the spirit/soul transitions to a different level. Once all the spiritual tasks are achieved to complete the nine levels of consciousness, the transition is then to Nirvana. In the Christian belief when one dies they go to Heaven or..... Well, that is one thought. Each of us has our own theory/philosophy of what happens when we die. Such a topic we all need to explore. It is the mourning of the loss of Gertrude, who should have been a Thanksgiving dinner over 4 years ago and got the reprieve to be in our little flock. Any kind of death stirs stuff in us about our own mortality. We can run the other way in fear or know that it is a transition. That one day we too will end the existence that we know as Now and..... It is up to each person depending on what he or she believes. When I died in 1980, after surgery, I felt nothing but peace as I was moving into the glowing, luminescent tunnel. I could see my body on the hospital bed. I watched as they rushed in and resuscitated me. Bang, I was back in my body. I really was very content to keep going into the tunnel. I was happy, no regrets. It was beautiful, welcoming and I had no fear. Today, I have no fear. It is all good. I do plan to stick around, though, for a while yet. I am cancer free as far as we know and that can change. So I enjoy as much of every day as I can, I experience as much of everyday as I can. This is what works for me. Enjoy, nap, play. Laugh a lot, walk a lot, do art a lot.

On the Journey: Whoosh. This is the sound of Angels' Wings heading to surround and support my dear friend Saundra in her passing. Please pray for Angels to help all those near the end of their lives to give them a peaceful and gentle transition. We all love our friend and her loss is a blow to her friends, family, loved ones and the local Art community. She fought the battle against cancer with her husband and the nasty bugger turned on her and consumed her energy, and has now ended her life as well. Send Angels, prayers of support and comfort for all families who are losing loved ones to this dreadful disease. This is a hard time. Another artist friend passed away week before last, losing her battle with Leukemia. Another artist and dear friend was recently diagnosed with breast cancer and is on her way to chemo and radiation treatments after her surgery. Another dear friend is fighting prostate cancer. I am mostly through my treatments but the Oncologist is making me take a break for this week so my skin can recover a bit for the last radiation treatments. This is a nasty disease that is a plague on us all. Somewhere I read that 1 in 8 women will develop cancer. I feel so sad for those who have to suffer with this disease, including myself. I am currently cancer free and I pray to stay that way to the end of my years, whenever that is. It is our lot in life to experience suffering through loss of friends, family and loved ones, as well as the assaults on our own health. Healthy living does not always prevent this disease; it can be genetic in origin. It can be from the environmental stressors, and more. So we have to figure out how to dodge the bullet, beat it and live to tell about it. One day at a time. Please pray for all of us valiantly fighting this battle for health; pray for the families who have loved ones who have lost the battle. I want to thank everyone for your Angels, prayers and support for all of us who have been affected by cancer. We are so lucky to be here. I find even with the loss, I can feel joy, I can feel alive, and I know those who have passed are still with us; everyday they are with us, in our hearts, free of pain and painting the Heavens. Thank you all for being in my life. Thank you for being you. Thank you for taking care of your Self, too. Be safe.

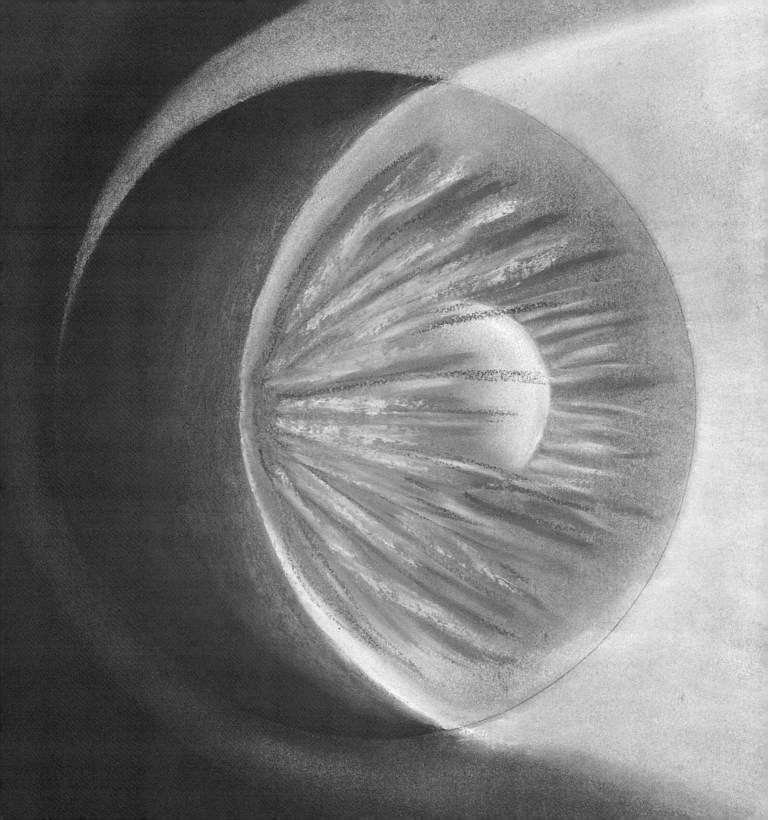

On the Journey: The Goddess. I rarely do images that are recognizable. Today seemed a good time to share the Goddess. The loss of a friend who lost her short battle is unsettling. The cancer had consumed her so fast because she ignored the symptoms and signs that she was in peril. She was so wrapped up in taking care of her husband, she put her needs and personal concerns aside. Sadly, it cost her her life. When one feels something is out of whack, check it out. Do something about it. Make sure it really is nothing; because if it is something and caught quickly, things can go a lot better. Don't put off the pap tests, the mammograms and the colonoscopies. Take care of yourself. No one else knows you, cares about you as much as you know yourself and need to care about yourself. I mourn the loss of my friend, a devoted artist, devoted wife and mother, as well as a great supporter of the arts in our area. I am so sorry for all of us who have lost their mother, their wives, their sisters or their friends to cancer today and every day. We need to take care of ourselves, allow the grief to flow and allow this to be the inspiration for some art to honor the lives lost. Thank you for your support for those who mourn the loss of loved ones.

On the Journey: Zapped #2: 24 years. One of the blessings of recovery is we get to honor our re-birthday, our sobriety birthday, into a new life without alcohol. I got my 24-year chip. Wow! I was not expecting the emotions that came up. Me, nearly speechless, amazing. Life does that to me lately. I feel more deeply, I probably express myself more deeply, as well. The Passion for "living in the now" brings about strong feelings. Life is rich, abundant and I am here as much as possible. Sometimes life is painful. Sometimes life is joyous. Sometimes I wonder why am I here, other times I know exactly why I am here: to share my passion, to learn, to be grateful for the very air I breath and for the very Earth I walk on. Sharing gratitude for this life is barely an adequate expression of how I feel after 24 years. I would not be here if I had stayed on that old road. I looked good on the outside but what was inside, well, shall we just say I am actually surprised that cancer took so long to appear in my body again. I treated my body so poorly for a majority of the first 41 years. So, 24 years is huge. I am grateful for the beautiful people in my life, I am grateful to live in such beauty. I am grateful for a good night's sleep. I am grateful for whoever put on the fireworks demonstration for the Fourth of July. It was great. Thank you to the workers who put on the show and helped people be safe. So, today is a special day in my life and I am grateful to be here, in the Now. Sober and present.

On the Journey: Verdant Energy. We often, in times of personal trouble, shut ourselves in. We withdraw. It is often difficult to engage when we feel depressed, depleted, not normal and/or under the weather. This, though, is the time we need to reach out, connect with friends. We don't want anyone to know, but we need to engage in life. I feel best when I am engaging with life or art. There are times when I would rather crawl into a hole and be left alone and I know that is the worst thing I could to do. During this Journey, there have been times when the quiet, alone time has been good, then I need to venture out. I am not sick. It is hard to describe actually how I feel. I am not my normal self yet, I am going through some profound changes inside. A friend sent me the following and I could not say it better: In an evening class at Stanford University the [last] lecture was on the mind-body connection - the relationship between stress and disease. The speaker (head of psychiatry) said, [to paraphrase] along with other things, that one of the best things that a man could do for his health is to be married to a woman; whereas for a woman, one of the best things she could do for her health would be to nurture her relationships with her girlfriends. At first everyone laughed, but he was serious. Women connect with each other differently and provide support systems that help each other to deal with stress and difficult life experiences. Physically this quality "girlfriend time" helps us to create more serotonin - a neurotransmitter that helps combat depression and can create a general feeling of wellbeing. Women share feelings whereas men often form relationships around activities. Women share from our souls with our sisters/mothers and evidently this is very GOOD for our health. He said that spending time with a friend is just as important to our general health as jogging or working out at a gym. There's a tendency to think that when we are "exercising" we are doing something good for our bodies but when we are hanging out with friends, we are wasting our time and should be more productively engaged. Not true. In fact, [he said] that the failure to create and maintain quality personal relationships with other humans is as dangerous to our physical health as smoking! So every time you hang out with a pal, just pat yourself on the back and congratulate yourself for doing something good for your health! We are indeed very, very lucky. So, cheers to our friendship with our friends. Evidently it's very good for our health. Thanks to all the women in my life who help me get and stay healthy, happy, and feeling very loved.

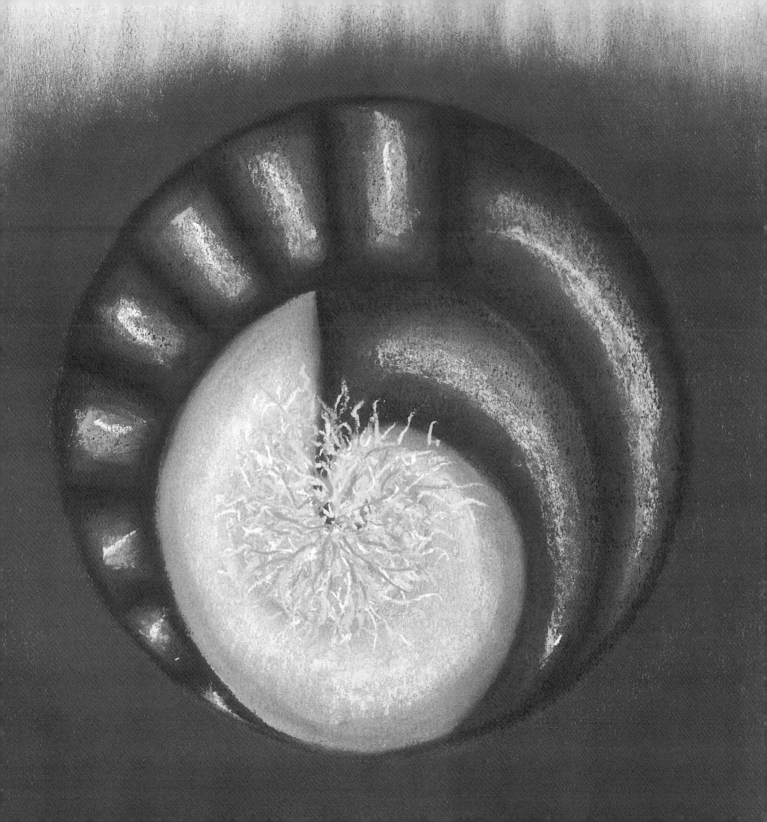

On the Journey: Life in Between. Today is another glorious day. My plans are simple today. No fuss, no muss, just R & R: clean the fish tank, finish the goose pool cleaning, nap, read in the sun and sip tea. Sounds like a good sunny day. The most important thing is to take care of me. So, to de-stress, I am doing water therapy by cleaning the tanks and pools, sitting in the sun, soaking up the vitamin D, napping and ignoring the rest of it. SELF CARE is essential. It is really calming to be in the space of feeling supported by the Universe. The way to get here is through mindfulness, meditation and breathing, just breathing. Letting the rest float by like the weather alert on the bottom of the screen, just let it go. This is the best path for me. So many things present themselves to my brain. I am looking at life as a gift, an adventure and a trial. Lessons abound, issues vary from small insignificant to grand, and then again, to grandiose. Experiencing the treatment for cancer has been a consciousness awakening process. I keep looking within, where am I today? Do I feel the same way about almost anything; life, death, friends, where I live, what do I want to do when I am finished with the treatments and what do I want to do when I grow up? Oops, I did say I was going to grow up? Why would I ever do that silly thing, being young at heart has lots of benefits. I still don't know who the old lady is in the mirror every morning, can't be me, I'm NOT that old, am I??? Funny, right? And I see my mother in that face, my Granny and my sister. We all have that look, but that can't possibly be me, I am not that...., well, I guess I am that old, outside. Inside is a whole different matter. The realization is that I had cancer. I am here, alive and enjoying this nice weather, being in the Now. The rest really doesn't matter because I am here right Now. My job today is to nap, do the compresses, laugh, play, enjoy the sunshine and enjoy just being. I hope you all can do the same.

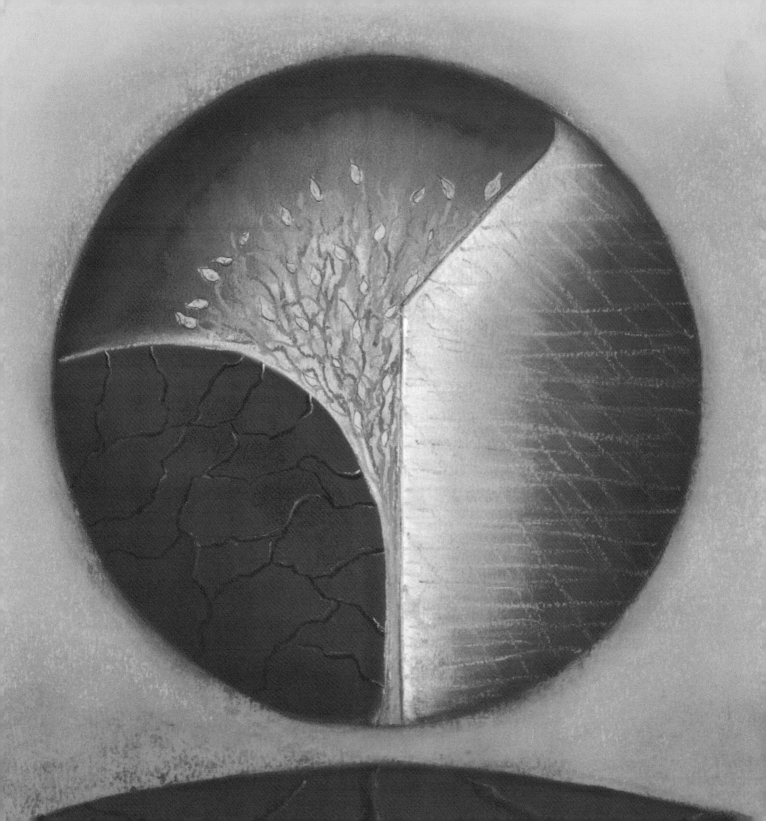

On the Journey: Bound in the Light. "Communication in interpersonal relationships is always a challenge" and is the topic of the day. During this time, getting radiation treatments, I have had to learn to keep my mouth shut, be quiet and not react because my fuses have gotten really, really short. The irritation level has been an issue: being tired all the time and being in constant discomfort. I have found by doing the art, being quiet, meditating and choosing not to jump right in, things are just a lot better. John has also had to struggle with his fears about cancer, having lost both his brother and sister to it. We have had a challenging time since the cancer diagnosis, then treatment; and John's own health issues. One day at a time. That is what we can do. I am finding that when I can put me aside and just listen to him, we do better, lots better! Try to understand that it is all in how we choose to "respond" to the situations, remarks or actions of whatever or whoever. WE choose. I can choose to "respond" to others' actions or not. My choice. I will say that since the cancer diagnosis, my responses are in line with what I consider being more grounded, centered and appropriate! That is to say, I leave my ego out of it more frequently. When someone says something negative, positive, or rude; I can choose not to take it personally. It's not about me, it is about them. Don Miguel Ruiz in <u>The Four Agreements</u> addresses this issue. I love the lessons in his books. Funny that it takes a life-altering event, like breast cancer, to make the four agreements sink in better. It is really strange how our puny little egos can get so thoroughly in our own way. I love observing myself making a choice: sometimes I catch myself in the old habit of taking stuff personally, and then stop and laugh. It is not about me. It is the other person's agenda, not mine. I can then let it go, with love and prayers. I am still practicing. I feel that I am getting better at seeing an opportunity to "Let IT go!"

My Gratitude List for today: I am grateful for the life I have, in the Now. I am grateful for the friends and family who have been so supportive. I am grateful for this place and the sunny days. I am grateful for the very air I breathe. I am grateful for today, right now. Thank you for being you, thank you for being here in my life.

On the Journey: Delicate Vessel of Life. We wallow in "things", wants, the past and the future. Yet we still ignore the most important experience we can possibly have: the here and now, in our body, consciously living in the present. This is really all that matters. I "constantly" quote Eleanor Roosevelt: "Yesterday is history, tomorrow is a mystery, today is a gift, that is why it is called the Present." The reason is to impress upon you, that we need to be in the Now. Experience the blessings, the challenges, the lessons and the gift of Now. Do not put off being you, the best you, you can possibly be, right now. I know I repeat myself at times but it is such a huge lesson we humans need to learn: "There is no time like the Present" to engage in the life we have Now. So for today, sit with your Self for 10 or 15 minutes, hear the chatter, put it aside and listen to your heart. Just 10 or 15 minutes is all it takes. You may hear that lovely sigh that says, you are here, you are listening to me. Thank you for this connection in the Now. Try it, see the blessings that come. Gratitude for that moment is the gift. Enjoy being with you in the Now.

On the Journey: Light at the End. "Perfectionism is the antithesis of creativity", (Lazarus). My circle is a little lumpy, HA HA HA. I love being a human with all the foibles and flaws, that I can actually admit being nothing more than a perfect human: flawed. The Great Spirit, The Great Creator, God, Goddess and All that Is, is perfection. We can revel in our humanness and honor our uniqueness in nature while living by Natural Law. One way to look at the path I have chosen is to see that an awareness has been evolving through this Journey. When we can look inside and see the beauty in us, in our work and our faith, we can find the Light within us, even in the darkest corners of our soul. The Light always is there; we need only to open our hearts to the power we have within, that is the conduit to our Higher Power. The Journey has deepened my faith in All That Is, each day. In this moment, being present is the greatest gift I have received. Living as if... and not missing out on the Now. With that said, I am off to do a "mowing meditation" on the big tractor. I have three fields to mow, about 5 or so acres. Not really that much and all pretty flat. The roar of the engine and the power of the mower to knock down the fields is a high. So, enjoy your day, I am nearly done with the radiation treatments. I am enjoying being me. Laugh, play, and take naps. So enjoy being you.

On the Journey: Understanding the Layers. With the last treatment coming up in a few hours, I feel the welling up of emotions. Relief is paramount. This has been a long Journey. It has made me look again at my mortality. Look again at the way I am living. Finding what is important and what I can let go. The mortality issue is interesting because, as I have said, I died following the first cancer surgery in 1980, even if it was only for moments. It changed my life. I was stepping into the tunnel of light, feeling safer than I ever had in my whole life. I started to change my way of thinking. It took awhile then, because I was not ready to give up my addictions that kept me unconscious. But coming out of that fog in 1987, and finally sober in 1989, my life took off like a missile into outer space, to a new faith in All That Is, to the new Me. I had to reconstruct me from the ground up. Today I am in this Life, Now, as much as possible. No, I don't do it perfectly, but I do get better at it everyday. I have all the time I need, for today. This is the most important thing. Sure, I get frustrated when things don't always go the way I want, but they go the way they are supposed to so I can learn whatever lesson, every day! Being open minded. Being able to take responsibility for me, my actions. This is where I am, open to changing, open to whatever comes one day at a time. Now is what I have and I am understanding this more and more. Life is a process, one day at a time. Enjoy your Self, play, laugh, and naps are good, too.

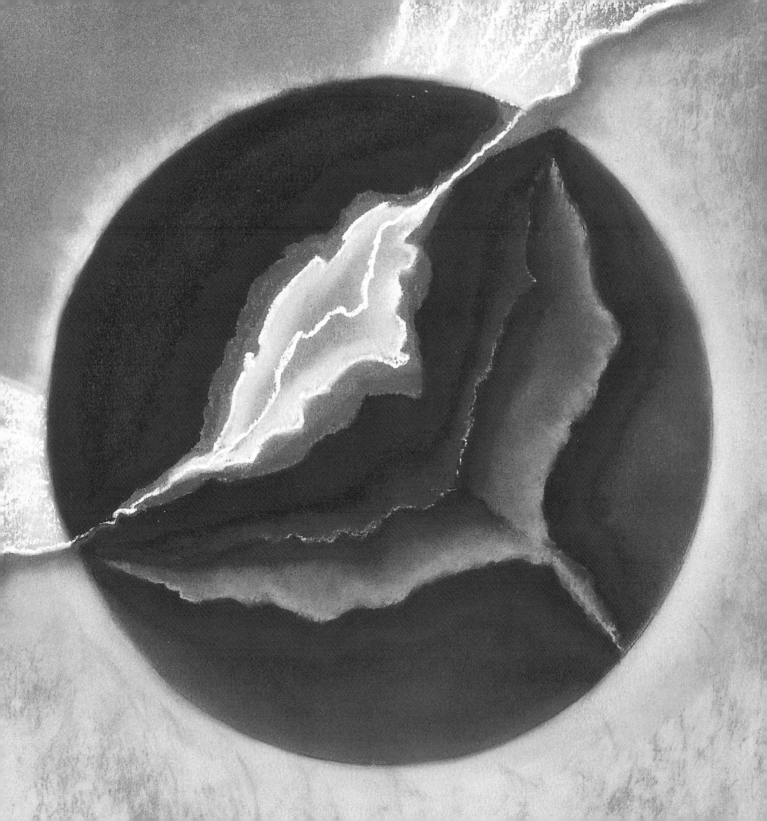

On the Journey: Grand Finale. The radiation treatments are a thing of the past. I got my Rad Grad Certificate. I am finished with this stage. Now, for the rest of my Life. I am here. I am alive. I am looking forward to this day's activities after a nap. I went to the 7 am meeting. I shared that yesterday was the last radiation treatment. I got rather choked up. Wow, out of nowhere, tears stung my eyes, a pile of emotions gushed over me, catching me unawares. So, now I face the new road and know I have a "few" things to do yet: I teach Intro to Art Therapy at Peninsula College during the Fall Quarter, I have new work and I will publish On the Journey.... and.... and Live every day like it is the last. Doing the very best to be me, to be true to my Self, to be honest with me and the world around me. On this Journey I have learned, among other things about my Self, that I am not alone. When I ask for Angels, prayers and support, there they are, filling my studio and my heart. This is a lesson for me, as well as others on their own Journey: You and I, we are NOT alone. There is a community of support right here, right now, whenever you or I need it. All we have to do is speak up, ask. I have learned that I have a very little, fragile girl inside who needs to know she is not alone, that others care about her, that others know she is afraid, afraid to ask, afraid no one will hear her fear, her need for help. This is the lesson. You and I, we are not alone. There is so much we take for granted about life until we are blindsided by illness or injury and we find we need help, support, prayers, sometimes a ride to the clinic and sometimes just the knowledge that someone is out there who cares. Thank you each and every one of you, for being here for me on this Journey. This Grande Finale is for this stage. Heaven knows what is next. So, I laugh, I cry, I take naps, I play and I heal. I pray you do, too!

On the Journey: Fervor. Four months after my last radiation treatment, my chest wall developed further problems that the medical people did not want to address. I went back to the surgeon, where she performed another biopsy. The cancer was back with a vengeance. The pain in my right chest wall area, under the mastectomy scar, had been escalating for weeks. It had developed a swollen, sore area that was turning purple and angry, while also developing a nasty undetermined rash. Really ugly. So the PET CT Scan was ordered.

The results: the cancer is in my bones, as well. I may never have been cancer free after all. This was the first scan, ever. They said it was not called for before. Medical prognosis is somewhat on the bleak side. That is the medical view and they leave out the most powerful healer we each have within our Self. Albert Schweitzer said: "Witch doctors (Shaman) succeed for the same reasons all the rest succeed. Each patient carries his own doctor inside him. They come to us not knowing this truth. We are at our best when we give the doctor who resides within each patient a chance to go to work". We have the doctor in us and I feel I kind of lost track of her on some levels.

I see this as an opportunity to create, to grow and thrive for however long I am able. The cancer does not dictate life. We have choices and so we make them now, to live to the fullest we can, in the here and Now. I choose to live, I choose to live on my terms and not be a slave to an incurable disease called life. I choose to use conventional medicine, and change my Spirituality practices along with changing my diet, exercising more and changing my attitude. These changes will get me through with the highest quality of life. Accepting what is and living is the most exciting path. I am doing the art for healing, for medicine and for the connection with Source, God, Goddess, All that Is that resides within each and every one of us. We need only to open our hearts and listen. The guidance is there, the healing is there and that is my path. I can choose to succumb to the pernicious spreading evil or I can choose to live to shed this dis-ease and find the ease in living again, with joy, with wonder and with love. One day at a time. I will listen with a respectful and an open mind. I will follow my heart of hearts, Source, the Great Spirit, God, Goddess, All That Is, and find the healing path for me, one day at a time. May each of us find a healing path that brings us peace and serenity in our heart.

About the Author

Since Cynthia Thomas was a small child she has worked in art. First and foremost she is an artist. Her training began when she was 8 years old, she has always thought of herself as an artist. Over the years, she has studied color theory and composition, and has worked with different media: drawing with pencil, pastels, charcoal; painting in oils and acrylics; printmaking, wood cuts; and sculpture, pottery and jewelry. She was privileged to have some very powerful mentors along the way. She earned a BFA from California College of Arts and Crafts and an MA from San Jose State University, both degrees in Metal Arts and Jewelry Design.

Ms. Thomas worked in the jewelry industry as a goldsmith, master model maker and in design research and development from 1971 to 1992. She has been creating bronze sculpture since 1992, which allowed her to create larger 3 dimensional pieces. In 2006 Ms. Thomas ventured into 2 dimensional artwork, using pastels. She started doing the mandalas on a daily basis as a challenge. They became a morning meditation, grounding her in the colors of the Chakras while processing emotions and feelings through the energies of the colors.

She has shown her artwork throughout the Western US, as well as New York, Chicago, in Galleries and at Fine Art Festivals. Ms. Thomas's work is in collections in the US, Europe, the Philippines and Australia.

In 1996, she earned a MA in counseling at University of San Francisco and in 1999 she completed a post-graduate Art Therapy Certificate from the University of California, Berkeley. Ms. Thomas found Art Therapy to be one path that brings changes to peoples' lives in a way that talk therapy does not achieve as well. New information in the neuroscience field is validating the efficacy of Art Therapy in changing the way the brain works: reducing stress, resolving conflicts, treating addiction, and helping those with PTSD eliminate symptoms and regain a more normal life. She practices as an Art Therapist, working on completing her hours for Board Certification.

If you have any questions. You may contact Ms. Thomas directly: Cynthia@MLCE.net.

Referenced/credited

Arrein, Angeles. The Four Fold Way: Walking the Paths of Warrior, Teacher, Healer and Visionary. San Francisco, Harper Collins Publisher, 1993

Cameron, Julia. The Artist's Way: A Spiritual Path to Higher Creativity. New York: A Jeremy P. Tarcher/Penguin, Penguin Putnam, Inc. 1992

Cassou, Michele. Point Zero: Creativity Without Limits. New York: A Jeremy P. Tarcher/Penguin, Penguin Putnam, Inc. 2001.

Cassou, Michele. Life, Paint and Passion: Reclaiming the Magic of Spontaneous Expression. New York: A Jeremy P. Tarcher/Penguin, Penguin Putnam, Inc. 1995.

Cornell, Judith. Mandalas: Luminous Symbols for Healing. Wheaton Ill.: Quest Books. 1994

Dale, Ralph Alan. Tao Te Ching: A new Translation & Commentary, Watkins Publishing, London, 2002

Gold, Aviva with Oumano, Elena. Painting From the Source: Awakening the Artist's Soul in Everyone. New York: Harper Perennial, 1998.

Judith, Anodea & Vega, Selene. The Seven Fold Journey: Reclaiming Mind, Body, Spirit through the Chakras, Freedom, CA. The Crossing Press, 1997

Moon, Bruce L.. Introduction to Art Therapy: Faith in the Product. Springfield, Ill.: Charles C. Thomas, Publisher, 2010.

Pipenburg, Robert. Treasures of the Creative Spirit: An Artist's Understanding of Human Creativity, Ann Arbor, Michigan, Pebble Press, 1998 & 2008

Ruiz, Don Miguel. The Four Agreements: A Toltec Wisdom Book, Amber-Allen Publishing, San Rafael, CA, 1997

Schneider, Michael. Beginner's Guide to Constructing the Universe: from 0 to 10: The Mathematical Archetype of Nature, Art, and Science, 1995.

Webster's II: New College Dictionary, Boston New York, Houghton Mifflin Company

CPSIA information can be obtained
at www.ICGtesting.com
Printed in the USA
LVIC06n2119260614
391847LV00002B/8

* 9 7 8 1 4 5 2 5 9 5 2 7 6 *